taste

derbyshire 2006/07

CW00371620

Welcome to the second edition of taste derbyshire, a food book brimming with all that's good about food in Derbyshire.

Not only does Derbyshire boast some of the most spectacular scenery in Britain it also produces, delivers and presents some of the finest food around.

We are delighted, in this years edition to present new recipes with food all prepared, photographed, cooked and eaten in our own kitchen. They are therefore tried and tasted! We thoroughly enjoyed them and we hope you do too.

This year we include local chefs presenting their favourite dishes for you to try at home. Also there are such tasty delights as Baked Apple Dumplings, Barnsley Chop with Baked Shallotts, Bloomers Original Bakewell Pudding, Derbyshire Honey Fruit Cake and many more mouthwatering dishes.

We are grateful to Royal Crown Derby for supplying all the china to present our food on. I am sure you will agree that they complement and enhance the dishes we show.

Last but not least we thank all who have contributed to taste derbyshire, the writers, advertisers, restaurants and the food and drink producers of Derbyshire including Chatsworth Farm Shop, Original Farmers Market Shop, Field House Foods and Mercaston Foods. We hope that you enjoy reading about yourselves and pick up some additional tips along the way from other contributors.

Jane, Garry and the team.

⌐⌐⌐⌐ David Burgess
Paul Timothy Smith
Victoria Isabella Plant

Editorial Assistant
Charlotte Elizabeth Burgess

The Cooking Team
James Cave
Jane Plant
Charlotte Elizabeth Burgess

Photography.
Jeanette Marie Howe
at Jen Photography 07793 739684

Design
David Robert Dykes
at Copper Dog Ltd
Luke Mellor

Printed by Buxton Press

Copyright Images Publishing Limited, Victoria House, Market Place, Crich, Derbyshire. DE4 5DD
Origination by Images Publishing Limited 01773
850050/850058

IMAGES
PUBLISHING

LIMITED

Victoria House,
Market Place, Crich. DE4 5DD 01773
850050/850058
www.tastederbyshire.co.uk

taste derbyshire contents

Meet the people

behind the scenes.

36 fantastic recipes

Bake an original

Bloomers
Bakewell Pudding
Pages 92-93

Top Derbyshire chefs
share with us their favourite dishes
and show you how to cook them.

Pages 100-119

See pages 120-147
for a comprehensive guide on:

Where to dine in Derbyshire.
Where to buy produce
and kitchen equipment

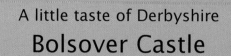

A little taste of Derbyshire
Bolsover Castle

Peak Ales

The Brewer's Tale

It all seems such a long time ago now, January, 2003. It had been such a carefully prepared plan – sell the house, uproot my family, leave secure jobs and set up a microbrewery in the Peak District! Simple.

'I thought I'd located an appropriate site in Bakewell but David Smith, my brewing consultant, had identified certain limitations. Knowing that I'd only one chance to get things right, I decided to find alternative premises. By chance, that day David and I had lunch in the Devonshire Arms, Beeley, and began chatting to the landlord, John Grosvenor. As he became aware of my intentions he suggested I enquire at Chatsworth. The Deputy Agent, Nick Wood, suggested that I take a look at Cunnery Barn on the Baslow to Chatsworth Road and to let him know if I thought it suitable.

I immediately drove to the barn. It is a road I had travelled along many times but I had never really noticed the barn. Night was just beginning to draw in and there was eerie calm about the buildings but their potential was obvious. I returned the next day to take a better look. The buildings were in disrepair and the site was terribly overgrown but it looked ideal for a microbrewery. I returned to the Estate Office to speak with Nick about the site. Clearly there were issues: planning,

electricity, drainage, renovation, finance etc. We decided that given the potential of the site it warranted a feasibility study at the least.

Eventually all the prerequisite approvals were in place and, in earnest, a site meeting was arranged and, just as everyone walked into the potential brew house, a barn owl flew out of the opposite window! There was clear evidence that a nesting box was in use and there was no alternative but to leave the site alone until all the young had fledged. By September the

Cunnery Barn

young birds had been successfully raised and renovation work on the barns could begin, including the building of a new nesting box. Rest assured, no other barn owls in Derbyshire have accommodation so grand!

Despite the delays the builders made good progress, and by Christmas nearly everything was ready for the arrival of the brewing vessels. Shortly afterwards, the stainless steel pipe work was in situ and the brewery was almost complete, a real contrast between the old and the new. Raw materials were ordered, and after a thorough clean we were ready to brew.

Virtually two years to the day after meeting Nick the first beer was brewed. It had been an emotional journey. Now I had to put into practice my business plan! The "proof of the pudding..." so they say. The initial recipes have been well received, and in our first year we have produced a stronger beer to add to the range - a Christmas special, "Noggin Filler", which has also gone down well.

The production of bottled beers was the next project for us, and we now have 'Bakewell Best' available through the Farmers' Market Shop in Bakewell, The Chatsworth Farm Shop in Pilsley, and Ibbotson's of Ashford. In addition we have signed up to the Direct Delivery scheme run by SIBA (The Society for Independent Brewers) and Enterprise Inns, and this will enable us to be found in more of Derbyshire's pubs!

Throughout our first year, we have had tremendous support from local landlords, and we would like to say 'Thank You' to them. We are now thinking about the way to develop the business, and we look forward to another, even better year to come!

When you are out and about do look out for Peak Ales – "Traditional Craft Ales Brewed on the Chatsworth Estate".

Robert Evans.

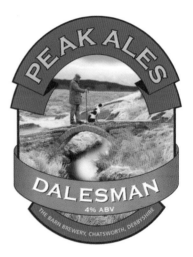

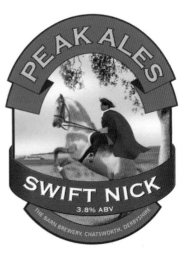

Herbs

for Everyone

Fresh herbs add flavour, colour, texture and vitality to any dish. Now they are readily available from supermarkets and delicatessens and from local Farmers' Markets. They can be bought as growing plants for the windowsill or garden or as packets of seeds to sow and grow on. "However you buy your herbs, you should use them in abundance", says Steve Croot of Field House Foods, a herb grower from Duffield, Derbyshire.

Perfect Partners

Certain herbs and foods make great partners, and are well established in cooking; chives with potatoes or eggs, dill with fish or cucumber, tarragon with chicken, basil with tomatoes, rosemary with lamb. Some starring herb partners include: thyme, marjoram and sage; and basil and oregano. Parsley goes with just about everything, and even seems to enhance the flavour of the herbs in its company. But why not experiment and develop your own specialities, by tasting as you prepare and cook a dish, you can tell if the flavours in the dish are as you want them to be? But remember the likes of oregano, sage, thyme, and rosemary are very pungent, so don't use too much at once.

Growing Herbs

Herbs are easy to grow and no garden should be without some. If you only have a small garden, you can grow herbs in pots or even in grow bags. Why not try growing thyme, rosemary, marjoram, parsley and chives in pots on windowsills. You should grow your herbs in a good quality potting compost, and should feed the plants with a liquid fertiliser to encourage good growth. Site them in a sunny/warm position and water frequently.

Preparation and storage

Rinse herbs in cold water and remove any discoloured leaves. Shake or pat with kitchen paper to dry before cutting with a sharp knife or scissors, or tear, in the case of basil.

To store herbs for later use, keep the stems intact and wash gently in cold water, being careful not to bruise the leaves or break the stems. Dry the herbs by patting them with kitchen paper. To keep them in prime condition, put them in a clean polythene bag with a sheet of moist kitchen paper, seal the bag and store in the salad box at the bottom of the refrigerator.

Alternatively place the herbs in a jar, their stems in water, and cover with a polythene bag. Store them in the refrigerator, and top up with water if required.

You can freeze any leftover herbs, such as mint or chives, by washing and drying them, wrapping them in foil or cling film. They will keep their flavour for about two months. You should use frozen herbs for cooking only, because while the freezing doesn't ruin the flavour, it does cause the leaves to become very limp.

When to add herbs

Bouquet garni and selected herbs are best added to long-cooking foods during the final sixty minutes of cooking. Add fresh herbs, with the exception of basil, to quickly cooked foods like pasta sauces and omelettes, along with the other ingredients. Basil should be added towards the end of cooking. Dried herbs are better soaked before being added. Add mint to green peas and potato dishes at the start of cooking, then add a few more sprigs at the end.

Field House Herbs
0141 416 1411

Jaquest

Food Specialist

In 1983 a former decorator and publican started a business in
Shutlewood, Derbyshire, smoking bacon and hams. His first
attempts were a disaster, but through dogged determination and
the will to succeed, John Jacquest has created one of the county's
premier delicatessens. Being self taught, John relied on the good
old adage "If I can eat it then it must be alright".

Customers flock from all over the UK to his shop, which lies in the shadow of Bolsover Castle. The
ground floor is an Aladdin's Cave of gastronomic delights. Award winning chorizo sausages, smoked
bacon, smoked roast salmon, smoked duck breast, ox tongue, pastrami, salt beef, venison and
kippers adorn the display cabinets.

John has won many awards for his great tasting food. The Guild of Fine Foods great taste awards awarded John Jacquest's homemade spicey chorizo the gold award for excellence, and many of his other products picked up silver medals. Gourmet loving customers feast their eyes on food that can only be classed as 5 star. Recently, John has started to supply upto 50 hotels and restaurants throughout Derbyshire, Leicestershire, South Yorkshire and North Nottinghamshire.

He prepares his foods such as hams, bacon and panchetta to his own recipe and says the secret of his success has been his determination to only buy the best products. His smoked salmon comes from the Shetland Isles of Scotland, and he uses Scottish Angus cross beef, and locally reared ducks and chickens. There are no chemical preservatives in his foods, he only uses natural wood smoke, sea salt, raw cane sugar and herbs & spices, creating quality British food that tastes as good as it looks. John is assisted by his wife Pauline, and their son Stephen, and they employ 3 part time staff to help with the huge demand from the catering trade.

Whilst John claims he has lost his sense of smell, due to the constant use of the smokery unit his ability to recreate such exotic dishes as the chorizo sausage, which he has even exported to Spain, shows that John has all the ingredients for a very successful business. A visit to his shop on Station Road, Bolsover is a must for all good food loving connoisseurs. Tel 01246 827972

A little taste of Derbyshire
Below the weir
Belper

The Honey Pot

The Honey Pot

A beekeepers diary

by Tony Maggs

Beekeeping covers many aspects, and here at The Honey
Pot we supply the public with our own products from our
apiaries, and the beekeepers with their equipment.
We can be spotted here in Derbyshire at certain events,
such as the Monthly Bakewell and Belper Farmer's Markets
and also at The Bakewell Show.
Our Derbyshire honey comes from the Peak District Moors
for the Heather Honey, and South Derbyshire for the
Spring and Summer honeys.

A typical year might go something like this.

January
The apiary inspections are restricted to making sure there is no damage from woodpeckers, who see the hives as 'square trees' and a place to attack for food. A check is also made for hive entrances blocked with snow. Prepare spare beekeeping equipment.

February
Check the weight of the hives by slightly lifting one side, this tells me if there is sufficient food, this time of year the bees can get very low on stores, so perhaps a feed of fondant might be needed.

March
Days are getting longer and on the warmer days we can see the bees foraging on the snow drops, crocus and hazel bringing home their vital early pollen for the developing larvae. Hive inspections include removing mouse guards and cleaning the floors.

April
When we have a warm day, now is the time of year for the first hive inspections, to check for egg, larvae and brood. Mark the Queen for ease of further inspections. The brood should be increasing rapidly and when nearly full we will fit the Queen excluders and the honey boxes ready for the early spring honey flow.

May
Regular weekly inspections to check for swarm control, prepare Queen rearing equipment ready for the demands from the local beekeepers after colonies of bees. Honey coming in can be from fruit trees, sycamore, dandelion and oil seed rape. Start the new nucleus hives and begin the first honey extracting from about the middle of May to prevent it from granulating in the frames.

June
Continue extracting until all of the early honey flow is over, also an inspection to monitor varroa control, weekly inspections continue and hive any swarms that might have escaped. Keep an eye on sufficient food in case of a "June Drop" when they can starve, as there can be as many as 40-50,000 bees in one hive, using up vital stores. Crops such as field beans can be coming in now. Make sure they have enough room by adding more honey supers if needed.

Prepare the colonies with travel screens and straps and take them to the Borage fields.

July

The main summer crop should be flowing in now such as clover, lime, willow herb, bramble and many more. The Borage is being extracted and Inspections continue but with less concern about swarming because most of the Queen rearing work is now done. Finally, the best hives are prepared and taken to the Derbyshire Moorlands in the Peak District to produce the best of all honeys, Heather.

August

Hot summer days and the heather is flowing well, wet days the bees stay inside and can starve, keep a check on the local weather forcast, regular visits to the moors to check that all is well.

September

Main summer honey extracting can now begin, then treat for the varroa mite and feed all of the colonies with enough food to see them through the next six months. Collect the hives from the Derbyshire hills and start pressing the Heather honey.

October

Enter the Derbyshire Honey Show at Carsington Water Visitor Centre, Apiary inspections include checking that all the hives have a good laying Queen, healthy brood area and the hive is packed full of food, protect against woodpecker attack, fit mouse guards and heavy rocks on roofs.

November

Continue selling our Derbyshire Honey at the local Farmers' Markets, store honey boxes and queen excluders, protect against wax moth.

December

Refine your cappings and make beeswax products such as candles, furniture polish and creams to give as presents. Check the hives have ample food.

The Honey Pot, Markeaton Park Craft Village, Derby. Tel: 01332 203893 www.localhoney.co.uk

Renishaw Hall Vineyard

Derbyshire's best kept secret

When Sir Reresby Sitwell sold his castle Montegefoni he lost the Italian vineyards that went with it, so he decided to plant vines at Renishaw.

The first trial plots were planted in 1973 in three different parts of the estate, the vines did best in the top paddock which were planted by the head gardener Andrew Smith, helped by the assistant gardener Ray Marples in the winter of '73-'74, 2,800 vines were planted. The first vines included Pinot Noir, Reichensteiner, Trebbiano and Seyval Blanc. At the time, the Renishaw vineyard gained an entry into the Guinness book of records as the most northerly vineyard in the world.

However, due mainly to poor vinicultural techniques the early vintages were disappointing, and many of the vine varieties proved unsuitable for our climate, with grapes grown in the 1911 greenhouse contributing a large share of each vintage. The fortunes of the vineyard changed when Sir Reresby met Mr. Tony Skuriat who was making excellent wines at his vineyard on the Nottinghamshire/Leicestershire border.

Mr. Skuriat took over the vinification process, i.e., from harvest, to bottle and recommended the planting of the vines Madeline Angevive and a new variety called Phoenix, alongside the sole remaining vine from the 1973 plantings, which were Seyval Blanc. This renaissance of the vineyard was accelerated with the appointment of a new head gardener in 1997.

A bottle from the recent record vintage - 2003.

David Kestevens
leading a guided tour
of the vineyard

The vineyard now consists of 800 vines of Seyval Blanc, 400 vines of Madeline Angevive and 300 vines of Phoenix. The record recent vintage was in 2003 with a harvest of 2,000 bottles, 200 were made into sparkling wine. It is hoped that as the new vines mature the total output of the vineyard may reach 3,000 bottles per annum.

In 2003 the UK entered the EU Quality and Regional wine scheme where UK wine has to pass both taste tests and chemical analysis to be granted Regional wine status (as opposed to UK table wine). Renishaw Hall wine has passed these tests, and can therefore be labelled 'English Regional Wine'.

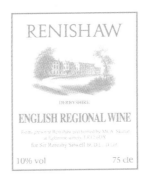

It is a light fruity wine, produced using traditional techniques and a live yeast. Best drunk slightly chilled on its own or as an accompaniment to fish dishes.

Renishaw Hall Vineyard, Renishaw, Near Sheffield S21 3WB
Tel: 01246 432310

A wine as unique and interesting as the estate from where it comes.

It's 4 o'clock, and in many households the china tea service will be making its appearance along with newly baked bread and butter, cucumber sandwiches and a range of tiny, fancy cakes.

But wait, it's totally dark outside, even the cat is still asleep, what is happening?

Apparently, there is another 4 o'clock in the day, a time when the bakers rise, a time to make dough for the bread to have with our afternoon tea, so what was I doing awake?

André Birkett had invited me to the Chatsworth Farm Shop's Bakery department to make some of their speciality breads. As I drove through the countryside not a soul stirred, the sheep in Chatsworth Park were still snoozing, but as I arrived at the farm shop I could see activity in the shape of Nick, one of the master bakers, who was going to put me through my paces.

The bakery produces over a dozen different types of bread and bread products daily, and every one of these breads must be on the shelves by 9.00am. Ready proved rolls were waiting to go into one of the five ovens that each week turns out thousands of tasty breads, cakes and confectionery.

Danny, a cheerful individual who dislikes golf, joined us! But not to be deterred, Nick and I had time to reminisce about our individual golfing achievements: that conversation didn't last long!

So on with the job in hand! Flour, salt, yeast and other ingredients had to be weighed out and, using the very latest in computer technology, each bread recipe was displayed on a digital screen, thus making the use of the good old fashioned recipe book obsolete. Each batch of dough was mixed, hand rolled and proved before it was placed in the oven.

Now the smell of fresh bread acts like a magnet, in fact many supermarket chains use the aroma of baking bread to attract customers into their stores. At Chatsworth Farm Shop the fresh baked smell is enhanced by the sight of real bread being packed and displayed only feet from the ovens.

Upper Crust!

Each batch of dough was
mixed, hand rolled and
proved before it was placed
in the oven.

Danny told me that after working for years in the bakery he has become immune to this wonderful aroma.

It was now 8am and other bakery staff were arriving, including Manager and Master Baker, Tony. Today he was making Battenburg cakes, but first he needed to make a batch of the very popular Victoria sponges.

CHATSWORTH

CHATSWORTH FARM SHOP

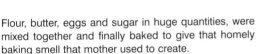

Flour, butter, eggs and sugar in huge quantities, were mixed together and finally baked to give that homely baking smell that mother used to create.

Whilst the cakes were being baked, I was told that in November, starting on the 24th, mince pies are produced, each one hand filled and each top hand rolled. By the 24th of December, 24,000 mince pies will have been baked and packed. 'Our visitors can't get enough of them' said Tony.

By 9.30am all the bread and the scones for the day had been baked. Now more batches of white bread cobs had to be made so they would be ready proved to be baked the following morning.

By now I was exhausted, the early start was beginning to take hold, so I departed for my office along with a selection of breads for the lads.

Twelve hours later, as I finish this article, I notice its nearly 4pm and time for afternoon tea: a cup of tea and a freshly baked fruit scone, compliments of my new found friends at Chatsworth Farm Shop Bakery, Nick, Danny and Tony.

taste Derbyshire would like to thank André Birkett and his staff, for making our visit a truly memorable.

J Cave

A Derbyshire Day

*by John Mitchell of Mitchell's Wines,
Meadowhead, Sheffield.*

Born in god's county Yorkshire, and proud of it, but I've been lucky
also having the added benefit of living just yards from Derbyshire
and the beloved Peak District. As a lad, in the school six weeks
holidays, day trips into the peaks was a special treat, having a shop
afforded few holidays so to be told the night before we were having
a day out was something else.

Catch the bus from Pond Street, in Sheffield, ticketed Fox House, clamber out with a packed lunch to wander down to marvel the great granite stone which was truly a toad's mouth, and trek just a little further to wonder the view that really was the surprise as you look down the Hope Valley to Hathersage and on.

I still enjoy all those things especially Bakewell and Chatsworth, but also the culinary delights the county offers. We started out as butchers, my father bought his meat from both Retford and Bakewell but always his lamb came from Derbyshire. It may be a Barnsley chop from the white rose, but Derbyshire lamb is the best our Country produces. There is only one wine to compliment in my book and that is Shiraz, renowned for its explosive blackberry flavours with hints of white pepper, often high in alcohol and usually gusty, the best is from Australia's Barossa valley, especially the old vine varieties.
Look out for the award winning wines of Peter

Lehmann, his Stonewell Shiraz being one of the best wines I've ever been privileged to taste, the 98 vintage being £28.50. I'm sure Chatsworth farm shop can supply the lamb if I bring the wine? Next in my shopping basket would be some smoked trout or salmon from my friends Jaquest Foods at Bolsover. For this we need a little Riesling, again I'm going Auzzie - Windy Peak Riesling. Riesling has been grown in Germany for thousands of years, floral medium style, Windy Peak is refreshingly dry, produced by the de Bortoli wine company founded in 1928, just named 'wine company of the year' and what's more their wines are going Stelvin. Stelvin, the innovation of the wine screw cap, which hopefully will put an end to corked wines, has come on so far in the last three years that even quality wines are getting capped, the latest being Chateau Bonnet entre deux mers, which would also go well with the smoked fish or even the lamb. For those preferring white wine, Chateau Bonnet is 45% sauvignon banc and 45% semillion, so don't say the French don't do interesting blends like the new world, they just don't put it on the label, well Bonnet is grassy and herbaceous with notes of granny smiths, apricots with toasted oak, clean and refreshing and resembles a sprite commercial with its crisp lemon lime finish, from Bordeauz entre deux mers between two rivers, the Garonne and the Dordogne.

It's time for desserts, Robert Walkers Tideswell herd of dairy cattle makes the ice cream, Brown Brothers winery makes the pudding wine, Muscat and Flora a unique blend to them - a flavour powerhouse bringing aromas of orange blossom to the nose and a fresh citrus hint to the palate, lovely jubbly, but if we haven't a sweet tooth it's the old cheese shop in Hartington for its renowned stilton, and what with that might you ask? Port of course. I could now fill ten pages on the virtue of port, the difference between bottled aged and wood aged ports, but why not a tawny aged in cask like a ten, twenty or even thirty year old, where the fruit and colour fade and the spirit comes to the fore, widely drunk in Portugal where the lighter style suits the climate, favoured by the wine trade in the UK, and equally as nice served chilled from the fridge.

Well, I can't fit much more into my day out in Derbyshire so it's back on the bus to Pond Street and good bye to the toad's mouth till another day.

Derby Markets

Derby Markets have been around for a long time. In 2004, they celebrated the 850th Anniversary of the granting of the Royal Charter for holding markets. The Charter gave the right to hold markets anywhere within the borough without interference. Over the years, Derby Markets have provided their customers with top quality food and goods at affordable prices.

This has been more evident in the last 20 years, with the major upsurge in supermarket sales. The market food traders have had to diversify by buying specialist foods for the many different groups of people who now live and work in the city, and purchase their supplies from all corners of the globe.

The selection of meats, fruit, poultry, cheeses and other foodstuffs on offer will stand comparison against any of the major supermarkets for quality, freshness and price. Indeed customers come from a 30-mile radius to Derby Markets to purchase their foods.

A LONG TRADITION OF PROVIDING QUALITY

The last few years have seen an increase in the number of specialist markets such as farmers' and continental markets. These have added to the attraction for shoppers in Derby, as they have now increased the variety of produce on offer, way beyond that of twenty five years ago.

Unlike many areas, Derby market traders were not opposed to the introduction of farmers' markets, as they felt that they would be of benefit to their own trade, by the introduction of specialist individual producers. This has proved to be the case. Some of the market stalls now stock items all year round, from the producers who stand on a monthly basis.

The farmers' markets are very well attended, and they enhance the general markets in Derby to the benefit of those people who shop in the city centre.

The same can be said for the continental markets, as they attract a different type of shopper into the city centre, who can then, perhaps, also sample the quality of the goods on offer in Derby markets for the first time.

Both the market traders and Derby City Council have invested considerable amounts of money to ensure that the markets can continue to provide quality at reasonable prices, in clean and well regulated premises.

A little taste of Derbyshire
Peveril Castle
Castleton

Start the day with your favourite tipple

The smell of freshly ground coffee is one of those aromas that acts as a magnet to the many pedestrians that walk along Chatsworth Road in Chesterfield.

Such is the fame of Northern Tea Merchants that thousands of visitors a year descend upon this exotic smelling shop that stocks teas and coffee from around the world. From the slopes of the mountains in Kenya to the plantations in South America, tons of coffee beans and great chests of tea from India and China, are imported by Northern Tea Merchants, stockists of the finest quality beans and leaves.

David Pogson and his son James are the driving force behind this hugely successful business started in 1959. After David canvassed the homes and businesses in and around Chesterfield the fame of his business grew and grew. Door step sales are still available, but many people believe that buying their coffee and tea from the local supermarket saves

Brazil Santos
A good 'middle of the road' type with a smooth, mild flavour

Ching Wo Tea
Ideal for afternoon tea with its bright copper infusion, light flavour and aroma

them money, however by careful blending and roasting at Northern Tea Merchants Brampton warehouses the consumer is guaranteed only the finest tea or coffee beans at a very competitive price. Huge machines produce 600 tea bags per minute, and the coffee bean roasting machine can roast up to 70 kilos at a time.

But which tea do you choose? Well with over two dozen kinds to choose from and the same number of coffees the best thing to do is to visit the shop and sample their vast range. This small family business has brought much pleasure to the coffee and tea drinking community in Derbyshire.

Earl Grey Tea
Flavoured with oil of Beramont it produces a delightful citrus flavour

For further information contact
David Pogson on 01246 232600.
Northern Tea Merchants
193 Chatsworth Road
Chesterfield

Gunpowder Green Tea
The tightly rolled grey-green leaves unfurl when infused and have a slightly fruity flavour

Fancy a
coffee?

These days if you ask for a coffee in a coffee bar, it usually results with a question about what kind of coffee you want? The choice is bewildering, espresso, cappuccino, latte and on and on in a seemingly endless list of Italian sounding names. It is not therefore surprising to think that coffee making was the sole province of the Italians, but try telling that to the Austrians and the Viennese in particular, for it is they with their tradition of coffee house society that makes them claim to have discovered coffee and its making.

The tradition of coffee houses in Vienna goes back many centuries, since 1683 in fact when the city was besieged by the Turks. The Turks were defeated and left in something of a hurry, leaving behind a few sacks of coffee beans. It did not take the canny Viennese long to work out what to do with their spoils of war and very soon the first coffee house was opened, beginning a great Viennese tradition.

Nowadays, coffee drinking is a way of life and some Viennese use their favourite coffee house as their postal address. Messages both over the phone or written can be left, but the waiters are also quite prepared to make excuses if one of the regulars is not supposed to be there at a particular time.

A visitor to a city which is strange to them should always try to observe local traditions and in Vienna coffee house culture has its own particular rules. Never on any account simply order a 'coffee', but work out in advance exactly what type of coffee you want, a problem not unlike that encountered in UK coffee bars. In Vienna coffee is not drunk out of cups, but out of bowls, each divided into different sizes of which the smallest is a 'Nusschale' (nutshell)', then a medium sized one called a 'Pikkolo', and for anyone needing more there is the 'Teeschale' (tea bowl), but do not ask for a 'Schale Tee' as you will get a bowl of tea!

Strengths and flavours are the next minefield to cross. If you want a mild, milky drink then ask for 'Schale Gold', but an 'Expresso' after a meal is very good taken either 'kurz' (strong), or 'gestreckt', meaning a weaker coffee made with more water. If however you want a stronger brew then you will need to order a 'Brauner' (brown), made with more actual coffee, or a 'Kapuziner', which has very little milk. Coffee cannot get much darker than a 'Schwarzer' (a black),

and a slice of cake

also known as 'Mokka'; 'Neger' (negro), is another name for this type of coffee, but if you are not on a diet then 'Kaffee mit Schlag' (coffee with whipped cream), is probably the most fattening.

As with all languages making an order can sometimes lead to embarrassment. Never ask for an 'Einspanner', or a 'Fiaker', as both mean black coffee served in a glass with cream, as well as meaning a horse-drawn carriage! Things are further complicated in a 'Beisel' (a type of small Viennese guest house), where should you order an 'Einspanner' you will get a sausage in a goulash sauce!

Archie's a great place to eat

The story goes that Colin and Debbie Reid the owners of the Glory Hole, the aforementioned butchers shop that now sells kitchens, fireplaces and furniture plus a whole range of other objects, decided to restore the barn that is attached to the rear of their shop. Colin designs and builds bespoke kitchens and restores antique furniture, so the skill and dedication to take on such a task were there in abundance. Now when the project of restoration was nearing completion, along came Lloyd and Rebecca Pearson who immediately saw the potential to realise their dream of opening their own restaurant. The rest, as they say, is history.

On the wall in this area you will notice a black and white picture of a young boy, Lloyds father, Arthur or 'Archie' as he was known, who sadly died June 2005 and is honoured with the restaurant's name. Archie shared the dream of Lloyd running his own restaurant with his brother and business partner Jason, who has contributed significantly in the creation of the interior of Archie's.

So what did we choose on the night?

To start, I ordered pan fried mussels in a wine and cream sauce, with dry cured bacon and shallots. Served in a hot iron pan, the presentation was excellent, as were the tasty delicate mussels complemented by the creamy sauce, which I took the opportunity of mopping up with the fresh bread that we had been served. My friend ordered warm walnut crusted goats cheese, two cakes of goats cheese wrapped in walnut! Did it work? Well yes it did! An interesting combination, that sent the senses on an adventurous trip through the soft cheese and crunchy walnut crust.

For main, one of our group ordered the herb crusted rack of Derbyshire lamb, nicely pink inside and subtly flavoured with the herb crust, the addition of a baby shepherds pie with the dish was nothing short of inspirational, an ingenious contrast! I chose to order the fish dish of char-grilled sea bass with battered crab.

Now, normally my first instinct is not to order fish, but I'm starting to see it as a challenge to try something new when dining out. Well I have to say that I really enjoyed the sea bass, cooked to perfection and so fresh tasting to the pallet, I can honestly recommend it. Another member of our group ordered the locally-farmed fillet of beef served with a single malt whisky sauce. How often do you order your steak medium rare and it comes out closer to well done? Well, the fillet was received exactly as ordered and the malt whisky sauce had a distinct but not overpowering taste.

For pudding, we each had a different choice. The traditional selection of British cheese and biscuits, an ample selection that would satisfy the largest of appetites, served on a slate tile, very aesthetic. The Baileys bread & butter pudding with butterscotch sauce! Can you remember bread & butter pudding, well this has a twist, if you like Baileys you'll love this! We also enjoyed duck egg crème brulee, a rich tasting desert particularly colourful made with local duck egg. But the winner for us was the open apple pie – apple pie but with no lid on it, ingenious!

The goal was always to have their own baby to run and I'm pleased to say that they have achieved it. It's a new restaurant, so there will be teething problems at first but Lloyd is very realistic about this and has the desire to get everything just right and will be.

Archie's Restaurant, The Barn, 4 Bridge Street, Sandiacre, Nottinghamshire NG10 4QT
Telephone 0115 949 9324
www.archiesrestaurant.co.uk

Amberside Farm Shop get greener!

As well as their excellent range of organic fruit and vegetables, some of the new foods they offer are: bread, butter, cheese, meat and poultry, Lime Tree Pantry Pies, ice cream, home-made cakes and preserves and an excellent range of store cupboard essentials. They also stock Ecover cleaning products and a personal care range.

Pentrich Lane End
Ripley, Derbyshire.
01773 512211

The National Forest Spring Water Company is an independent company bottling water from a source 220ft below ground in gravel beds. Geological studies have shown that these gravel beds could have been laid down by a river of the past.

Taste the
water

The site of The National Forest Spring Water Company is on the outskirts of the historic Derbyshire town of Melbourne within the National Forest. Even the name Melbourne is associated with water as the name has been derived from 'mill on the brook'. The town is situated 2 miles from the River Trent. A few miles upstream this waterway continues to be used in the production of the famous beers at Burton-on-Trent. The land surrounding Melbourne has a history of market gardening and the water now used for spring water production was originally used to irrigate the salad and vegetables grown in the surrounding fields.

All their products are naturally pure English Spring Water bottled direct from source, on site, using state of the art facilities. They include still, sparkling or Forest Fruits flavoured. Many recent studies have shown the benefits of drinking pure Spring Water whether at home, office or school.

More recently they formed a sister company The National Forest Vending Company to specialize in providing a full water cooler system, again using pure Spring Water, aimed at environments where a constant supply of fresh cool water in not only pleasant but a real health benefit for all to use.

Why not give
taste derbyshire as a

gift

Visit our website
www.tastederbyshire.co.uk
for details

The perfect farmhouse breakfast...

Since opening its doors 5 years ago The Original Farmers Market Shop has become established as the by-word for fresh, locally produced food.

The shop is open 7 days a week. The philosophy of the shop is still the same in that they source within a 30 mile radius however, they now also go further afield while still maintaining their principles of knowing their producers and their products.

...or just something different for supper

Carolyn has now join Richard as a partner and has brought with her the business experience from a blue chip company and her passion for baking and creating new recipes for the shop. Richard and Carolyn now have competition between themselves as to who can come up with an original recipe.

Says co-owner, Richard Young: 'People travel from all over the country just for our bacon - our dry-cured bacon and boiling hams are from Gloucester Old Spot and Saddleback pigs bred by Sherwood Forest Farm, they taste like real bacon and ham should! We have exotic meats such as crocodile plus more local to home haslett and game - rabbit, hare, quail, guinea fowl, pigeon and our famous 3 bird roast.'

There are sausages of every flavour imaginable (including gluten-free) and Mistlehall Farm's antibiotic-free, free-range eggs which are produced by heather–grazed and springwater-fed hens which are delivered direct from the farm. Add fresh, preservative-free bread baked daily by a new local bakery and a selection of home-made jams and marmalades, and you have the perfect farmhouse breakfast!

If you are looking for something special for a dinner party there are delicious and unusual

smoked meats and fish and a wide variety of game. Locally reared, rare breed and organic pork, beef and lamb and free-range chicken are also on offer.

They have increased their range of cheeses to in excess of 50 different varieties from around the country including Hartington's Blue Stilton and the Stafforshire Cheese Co.'s Cropwell Bishop and Colston Bassett. As well as a range of organic cheeses, there are sheep and goats' cheese and the more unusual flavoured 'walnut and pepper' and 'garlic' cheese from Franjoy Dairies.

The shop now has over 11 local breweries and has been recognised by Camra for their extensive range of real ales including Peak Ales and Thornbridge. 'A good cheese should be served with a good ale' says Richard, 'and you will certainly find some of the best ales in the county right here, from the strong and dark Porter by Burton Ales to the light and hoppy, award winning 'Easy Rider' by Kelham Island or the quirkily-named 'Leatherbritches', you will be sure to find something to your taste'.

New to them is the gluten free range which now has pork pies, quiches, pizzas and meat pies. All of them you will find in their main range as well as ready meals and, not forgetting, the original Bakewell pudding!

Too busy to cook? Try the tempting range of ready meals such as Glynis Maycock's Liver and Onions and Duck in Plum Sauce. The pie range has grown from steak and kidney to exotic pies such as: game, rabbit, partridges, pheasant, wild boar, venison and ostrich, which are all home made. Carolyn keeps adding to the range with pies like: fidget, duck and orange and lamb crumble. They make their own pork pies - made from their own recipe. These can be frozen or cooked and are ready to serve in minutes. There is an exquisite range of pies, cooked or oven-ready, as well as small pies and pasties for the hungry shopper! To compliment their pies, try their home-made gravy.

For the sweet tooth, the selection of home made chocolates and puddings will prove irresistible. They have an extensive range of cakes, including gluten free and sugar free. 'Kiwi and mango' cheesecake, roullades, angel cakes and the favourite lemon meringue pie jostle with sticky toffee pudding and home-made dairy ice cream to tempt you for that special treat. They now stock six varieties of Bakewell tarts and puddings.

Friendly, knowledgeable staff are always on hand to help you in your choice. Says Richard 'As most of our suppliers are small, specialist producers, it's always worth phoning to check on availability of specific items. We will happily take orders in advance for dinner parties and special occasions. We also provide complete out-side catering. We take regular weekly orders by mail-order, by internet, E-mail, post or phone and have them boxed, ready for collection. We are constantly looking for new and unusual products – we will always try to find a supplier in response to a request'.

If you want assurance that you are buying environmentally friendly, local produce or you're just looking for something different for supper, The Original Farmers Market Shop is well worth a visit.

The Original Farmers Market Shop, Market Street, Bakewell. Telephone: 01629 815814

The Q Butchers Guide

How do we guarantee that the beef, pork or lamb that we cook will turn out correctly cooked? The Guild of Q Butchers provides some interesting guidelines into cooking that Sunday lunch or an informal al fresco barbeque. Below are the basic cooking times and tips for beef, lamb, pork etc.

COOKING TIPS FOR BEEF AND LAMB
(credits to EBLEX - www.beefyandlamby.co.uk)
There are many delicious ways to cook Quality Standard beef and lamb.
This section gives you great tips on how to cook beef and lamb successfully whichever way you choose to cook it.

Meat storage and preparation
Ensure that hands, equipment and surfaces are scrupulously clean before and after
handling food and between handling raw and cooked foods - especially when using
the barbeque.
Check your fridge is operating at the correct temperature: between 0 and 4 degrees centigrade.
Keep a separate hard, durable chopping board for preparing raw meats.
Defrost frozen foods thoroughly (unless otherwise stated) and do not re-freeze once thawed.
Cover and store raw and cooked foods separately. Store uncooked foods lower in the refrigerator than cooked ones.
Make sure foods are thoroughly and evenly defrosted, and when re-heating ensure piping hot throughout.
When marinating meat, cover and store in a refrigerator.
Ensure burgers and sausages are thoroughly cooked and piping hot before serving.
When roasting a stuffed joint remember to weigh the joint after stuffing, then calculate the cooking time.

Food thermometers can be used to ensure internal food temperatures are sufficiently hot.

Stir-frying
Stir-frying is an ideal quick method of cooking meat as the thin strips cook in only a few minutes.
It is only necessary to use a very small amount of oil (1 tablespoon) when stir-frying. Use a vegetable based oil which can be heated to higher temperatures.
Use a non-stick wok or large frying pan. Always ensure that the pan or wok is really hot before adding the meat a little at a time - it should sizzle when the pieces are added.
The meat should ideally be trimmed of excess fat and cut into approximately 1cm (1/2") strips, cut across the grain to help tenderise the meat and prevent shrinkage.

Method
Heat 15ml (1tbsp) oil in a wok or large frying pan.
Add the meat and stir-fry for the recommended time.
Add the hardest vegetables first (e.g carrots, onions) and cook for 2-3 minutes before adding the rest.
Add sauce (up to 150ml(1/4pt)) and cook for a further couple of minutes.

Guide to roasting
Roasting doesn't need to be complicated. Simply weigh the raw joint and calculate the cooking time using the table below to ensure the meat is cooked to your liking.

To Cooking Meat

Roasting essentials

Position the oven shelves so the meat is in the centre of the oven.

Place the joint uncovered on a wire rack in a roasting tin ensuring any fat is on the top. This allows the juices to run down and baste the joint naturally.

When roasting beef and lamb joints, the secret is to cook the joints in a moderate oven for slightly longer to ensure even cooking.

Remember to weigh beef and lamb joints before calculating your preferred cooking time.

Allow the joint to rest for 5-10 minutes after cooking to let the meat fibres relax and juices distribute evenly so the joint is moist and easy to carve.

The degree of cooking can be tested easily using a meat thermometer towards the end of the cooking time: insert into the centre of the joint or at the thickest point, until it reaches the required temperature.

Beef: Rare - 60°C, Medium - 70°C, Well Done - 80°C
Lamb: Medium - 70-75°C, Well Done - 75-80°C

Roasting in liquid

Slow moist methods include pot roasting, stewing, braising and casseroling. These methods are ideal for tenderising less expensive, less tender cuts of meat and are convenient ways of cooking as they require very little preparation or attention during cooking. Simply pop one in the oven or on the hob and let it cook while you sit and relax.

As it is all cooked in one pot you'll save on washing up too!!

Pot roasting

Pot roasting uses whole joints of meat - boned and rolled joints are ideal for pot roasting.

It is traditionally carried out by browning the joint and then cooking in the oven or on the hob with liquid and vegetables.

Allow approximately 450g(1lb) vegetables (use root vegetables cut into large pieces) and 150ml(1/4pt) liquid (try stock, wine, cider, beer etc) for a 1.25kg(2½lb) joint.

Method

Heat 15ml(1tbsp) oil in a large heavy based saucepan or casserole dish. Brown the joint on all sides.

Add the vegetables and liquid, and any seasoning or herbs.

Cover and cook either on the hob on a low simmer or in the oven for the calculated cooking time.

Stewing, braising and casseroling

Stews and casseroles use cubed meat, while braising traditionally uses whole steaks or chops. As with pot roasting the meat is simmered at a low temperature on the hob or in the oven with added liquid.

Allow approximately 225-350g (8-12oz) vegetables (use root vegetables cut into chunks) per 450g(1lb) meat and 150ml (1/4pt) liquid (try stock, wine, beer etc).

Method

It is not necessary to pre-seal the meat first, just add all the ingredients to a large pan or casserole dish, cover and cook for recommended time.

You could also try adding jars of shop bought sauces to make preparation really quick. This method is ideal for making tasty curries, simply add a jar of shop bought curry sauce to some cubed meat and vegetables and cook for the calculated cooking time.

Barbeque tips

Light barbeques well in advance, making sure you use enough charcoal, and wait until it is glowing red (with a powdery grey surface) before starting to cook.

Keep meat refrigerated for as long as possible before cooking.

Make sure the chef doesn't mix up the cooking utensils, boards or plates for raw and cooked meats - keep them separate.

Always wash hands thoroughly - before preparing food, after touching raw meat and before eating.

Ensure all sausages and burgers are thoroughly cooked before serving (juices should run clear).

Pan-frying

Pan-frying, or 'shallow frying' is a quick cooking method for small, tender cuts using an uncovered pan on the hob.

Use a heavy-based frying pan, sauté pan or wok. For best results, use only a small quantity of oil or butter.

Ensure that the oil is hot before adding your preferred beef or lamb cuts.

Sear each side quickly to seal in juices and retain succulence.

Only turn your steaks once during cooking; leaving them to cook untouched will produce juicier results.

Grilling

A fast, dry alternative to pan-frying for cooking tender cuts, using intense radiant heat either above or below the meat. Char-grilling or barbecuing seals the meat juices by forming a crust on the surface of the meat. The meat must be basted with a prepared glaze, butter, oil or reserved marinade mixture. This gives a distinctive flavour to your beef or lamb and keeps the meat moist and succulent. Only turn your steaks once during cooking; leaving them to cook untouched will produce juicier results.

Under The Heat.

Cook the food under a heated element such as a conventional electric or gas grill.

Over The Heat.

Brush the meat lightly with oil and ensure that the grill rack is pre-heated. Place the grill rack over gas or charcoal grill or barbecue.

Between Heat.

Place the meat between heated grill bars (such as vertical toaster or grill.) This employs radiant heat, convection heat or both.

Baking

This method employs dry cooking in the oven – either in a roasting tin or in a sealed container or foil 'packet'. For wonderfully tender meat, choose a clay or terracotta 'brick' which effectively creates a clay oven within your oven. As the oven heats, steam condenses in the pot, basting the meat in its own juices. The end result is moist, tender, full of flavour and naturally cooked with no extra fat.

Basic Recommended Cooking Times

Pork 375°F/190°C, Gas Mark 5 – allow 30 to 35 minutes per lb (450g) plus 30 minutes.

Beef (A)= hot oven – suitable only for prime cuts. Set oven to 425°F/220°C, Gas Mark 7.
(B)= moderately hot oven – suitable for all joints. Set oven to 375°F/190°C, Gas Mark 5.
Rare – 15 minutes per lb (450g) plus 15 minutes at (A); 20 minutes per lb (450)g plus 15 minutes at (B).
Medium rare – 20 minutes per lb (450g) plus 20 minutes at (A); 25 minutes per lb (450g) plus 20 minutes at (B). Carve slices from outside of joint for people who like beef well done.
Well done – 25 minutes per lb (450g) plus 25 minutes at (A); 30 minutes per lb (450g) plus 30 minutes at (B).
Cook joints with a natural fat with fat side uppermost, add a little fat to lean joints. Baste during cooking or use covered roasting time.

Lamb 375°F/190°C, Gas Mark 5. Allow 25 to 30 minutes per lb (450g) plus 25 to 30 minutes over. A piece of lamb on the bone will cook more quickly than one without.

Turkey 425°F/220°C, Gas mark 7 for one hour then 375°F/190°C, Gas Mark 5. Allow 15 minutes per lb (450g) plus 15 minutes over. To test if cooked, insert knife where leg joins body; juice must be colourless, not pink.

Goose/duck 425°F/220°C, Gas Mark 7 for one hour, then 375°F/190°C, Gas Mark 5. Allow 20 minutes per lb (450g) and 20 minutes over.

Ham/gammon Cook with water or your preferred mix. Simmer for 20 to 25 minutes per lb (450g) plus 20 minutes. If serving cold gammon, allow to cool while still in the liquid.

A little taste of Derbyshire
Hardwick Old Hall

Beekeeping

in the Peak District National Park

The varied landscape of the Peak District and Derbyshire boast an abundance of very varied wildlife habitats and agricultural land which makes it an ideal environment in which to keep bees. The mixture of Gritstone and Limestone, high moorland and deep valleys ensure that sources of pollen and nectar can be found from early spring when the first garden snowdrops appear to late Autumn when the heather is in full bloom.

Beefarming in this area is dependant on some key crops to ensure that a business is viable – from around Easter farms on the low ground around Derby and Ashbourne grow oilseed rape – although not always a popular honey rape honey provides a good start for the bees, to enable colonies to build up in number and begin to store food for themselves ready for the next winter. Wildflower hay meadows provide work for the bees through the main part of the summer.

By the end of July in most areas beekeepers have seen the bees complete their years work and begin to prepare the colonies for the winter – not so for hard working Derbyshire bees – they have one more crop to collect before settling down to sit out the winter – the heather comes into bloom during the last week of July and first weeks of August – the bees must be in good condition and strong to collect this premium crop. The hives are moved close to the heather to minimise flying time and so help the bees to maximise the flying time available. The fickle weather at this time of year can have a massive impact on the amount of honey produced which can vary from year to year.

Mark Dennison, Daisybank Apiaries. 01298 83526

tasty recipes
for you to try

Frozen Melon

Serves 6

Ingredients

50g Unrefined Caster Sugar
30ml Clear Honey
15ml Lemon Juice
60ml Water
1 Medium Cantaloupe Melon or Charentais
Melon, about 1kg
Crushed Ice
Cucumber Slices
Borage Flowers

Method

1. Put the sugar, honey, lemon juice and water in a heavy pan, and heat gently until the sugar dissolves. Bring to the boil for 1 minute without stirring to make syrup. Leave to cool.

2. Cut the cantaloupe melon in half and discard the seeds. Carefully scoop out the flesh using a metal spoon or melon baller and place in a food processor, taking care to keep the halved shells intact.

3. Blend the melon flesh until very smooth, then transfer to a mixing bowl. Stir in the cooled sugar. Invert the melon shells and leave them to drain on kitchen paper for a few minutes, then transfer them to the freezer while making the sorbet.

4. If making by hand, pour the mixture into a container and freeze for 3 - 4 hours, beating well twice with a fork, a whisk or in a food processor, to break up the ice crystals and produce a smooth texture. If using an ice cream maker, churn the melon mixture in the ice cream maker until the sorbet holds its shape.

5. Place the sorbet into the melon shells and level the surface with a knife. Use a dessertspoon to scoop out the centre of each filled melon shell to simulate the seed cavity. Freeze the prepared fruit overnight until firm.

6. To serve, use a large knife to cut each melon half into three wedges. Serve on a bed of ice on a large platter or individual serving plates, and decorate with the cucumber slices and borage flowers.

Penne with Cream and Smoked Salmon

Serves 4

 Ingredients

350g Dried Penne
115g Thinly Sliced Smoked Salmon
2 - 3 Thyme Sprigs
30ml Extra Virgin Olive Oil

150ml Extra Thick Single Cream or Soya Cream
Sea Salt and Ground Black Pepper

 Method

1. Cook the dried pasta in a large pan of lightly salted boiling water for 10 minutes, until it is just tender.
2. Using sharp scissors cut the smoked salmon slices into thin strips, about 5 mm wide. Strip the leaves from the thyme sprigs and rinse them thoroughly in cold water.

3. Drain the pasta and return it to the pan. Add the oil and heat gently, then stir in the cream with about one quarter of the smoked salmon and thyme leaves, then season with pepper. Heat gently for 3-4 minutes, stirring all the time. Check the seasoning. Divide the pasta among four warmed bowls, top with the remaining salmon and thyme leaves and serve immediately.

Potato and Turnip Soup

Serves 6

 Ingredients

100g Turnip, peeled
100g Vegetable Marrow flesh
100g Potato, peeled
40g Butter
500ml Water
500ml Milk
Salt and Pepper
4 Leaves of Chard or White Beet, shredded
25g Vermicelli
6 Sprigs of Chervil

 Method

1. Cut the vegetables into small square or round slices and cook them gently with the butter.

2. Add the water and milk, season and when the vegetables are half cooked, add the shredded leaves of chard or white beet.

3. About 15 minutes before the soup is cooked, sprinkle in the vermicelli. Garnish each bowl with a sprig of chervil.

Barnsley Chops
with Baked Shallots
and Parsley

Serves 4

Ingredients

500g Shallots, unpeeled
4 Barnsley Chops, each about 200g
100ml Lamb or Beef Stock
Good Knob of Unsalted Butter
1 Tablespoon Chopped Parsley
Sea Salt and Freshly Ground Black Pepper

 Method

1. Preheat the oven to 200°C. Put the shallots, still in their skins, on a roasting tin and bake for 45 minutes. Leave them to cool then top and tail them with a sharp knife and gently squeeze the onions out of their skins.

2. Heat a lightly oiled griddle pan to its hottest. Season the chops with salt and pepper and grill for 4- 5 minutes on each side for rare or 7 to 9 minutes for medium.

3. Put the shallots into a frying pan with the stock and cook on a high heat to reduce the stock until it is almost evaporated. Add the butter and chopped parsley, lightly season with salt and pepper, and stir until the butter has melted into the liquid to form a glaze.

4. Place the chops on warm plates. Spoon the glazed shallots on top, or serve them separately.

Roast Beef and Yorkshire

Serves 4 to 6

 Ingredients

1 Rib of Beef on the bone
Beef Dripping or Vegetable Oil
2 Onions, peeled and halved
2 Carrots, scrubbed or peeled
and halved
Sea Salt and Freshly Ground
Black Pepper

For the Yorkshire Pudding
250g Plain Flour
4 Medium Eggs, beaten
500ml Milk

For the Gravy
Glass of Red or
White Wine
200ml Beef Stock

 Method

1. Heat the oven to 220°C. Put a little dripping into a large roasting tin and heat in the oven for 10 minutes. Season the beef and roast for 15 minutes, turn it over to seal the meat and keep the juices in. Put the onions and carrots under the beef to act as a trivet, this helps the beef to cook evenly and flavours the gravy. Allow 30 minutes per kilo for rare and add another 10 minutes per kilo for medium. Baste the meat regularly with pan juices.

2. To make the Yorkshire batter pour the flour into a bowl and add a good pinch of salt. Mix in the eggs and a little of the milk with

...udding

*Of all the flowers
I like the best*

the rose it is a good'n.

*But give to me the
flour that makes*

*the good old
Yorkshire pudd'n.*

a whisk to form a paste. Mix in the rest of the milk, trying not to beat the batter too much, to give a thick pouring consistency.

3. 25 minutes before the beef is ready, pour some of the hot fat from the beef into individual Yorkshire pudding tins and heat in the oven for 5 minutes until smoking. Pour the batter into the roasting tin and bake for 30 minutes, or until well risen and crisp.

4. Rest the beef for about 15 minutes before carving.

5. To make the gravy, deglaze the roasting pan with the wine and add the stock. Simmer for 2 minutes while stirring.

Sirloin Steak with Avocado and Chilli

Serves 4

 Ingredients

4 Sirloin Steaks
4 Caribe or Mild Red Chillies
1 Tablespoon Extra Virgin Olive Oil
Salt and Freshly Ground Black Pepper
8 Vine tomatoes - skinned and chopped

For the Guacamole
2 Ripe Avocados, halved
$1/2$ Medium sized White Onion, peeled and finely chopped
$1/2$ Caribe or Mild Red Chilli, finely chopped
3 Heaped Tablespoons roughly chopped fresh Coriander Leaves

Method

1. Cut the top off each chilli and remove the seeds, cut each chilli into 4 long slivers. Place on a foil lined grill pan under a preheated grill for about 1 - 2 minutes, or until the skin just starts to brown and the flesh starts to soften. Remove and allow to cool.

2. Make 4 one inch slits into the edge of each steak to form four little pockets. Stuff each slit with a sliver of chilli. Season each steak with freshly milled black pepper.

3. Heat the oil in a large heavy based frying pan until very hot, you should be able to really smell the olive oil and you will see tiny bubbles. Place the steaks in the oil and cook over a high heat for 2 minutes, then turn and cook for a further 2 minutes, still on a high heat.

4. Turn the steaks back on their original side and continue cooking until they are done to your liking, another 3 minutes for rare, 5 to 6 minutes for medium and 8 to 10 minutes for well done.

5. Mix the chopped onion and chilli for the guacamole with the coriander and salt in a pestle and mortar. Scoop the flesh of the avocados into the bowl and mash everything together with the pestle. The texture should be slightly chunky.

6. Taste for seasoning and stir in the tomatoes.

7. Serve on warmed plates and sprinkle with salt. Top with a generous spoonful of guacamole and serve.

Steak, Mushroom and Ale Pie

Serves 4

 Ingredients

30ml Olive Oil
1 Large Onion, finely chopped
115g Chestnut or Button White Mushrooms, halved
900g Lean Beef in one piece
30ml Plain Wholemeal Flour
45ml Sunflower Oil

300ml Stout or Brown Ale
300ml Beef Stock
500g Puff Pastry
Beaten Egg to glaze
Sea Salt and Ground Black Pepper
Steamed Organic Vegetables to serve

 Method

1. Heat the olive oil in a large flameproof casserole dish, add the onion and cook gently, stirring occasionally for about 5 minutes. Add the halved mushrooms and continue to cook for a further 5 minutes, stirring occasionally.

2. Meanwhile, trim the meat and cut it into 2.5cm cubes. Season the flour and toss the meat.

3. Use a draining spoon to remove the onion mixture from the casserole dish and set aside. Add and heat the sunflower oil, then brown the steak in batches over a high heat to seal in the juices.

4. Replace the vegetables, then stir in the stout or ale and stock. Bring to the boil, reduce the heat and simmer for about 1 hour, stirring occasionally. Season to taste and transfer to a 1.5 litre pie dish. Cover and leave to cool. Preheat the oven to 230°C.

5. Roll out the pastry in the shape of the dish and about 4 cm larger all around. Cut a 2.5 cm strip from around the edge of the pastry. Brush the rim of the pie dish with water and press the pastry rim with beaten egg and cover the pie with the pastry lid.

Press the lid firmly in place and then trim the excess pastry from around the edge of the dish.

6. Use the blunt edge of a knife to tap the outside edge of the pastry rim, pressing it down with your finger as you seal the steak

and mushroom filling into the dish.

7. Pinch the outside edge of the pastry between your fingers to flute the edge. Roll out any remaining pastry trimmings and cut five or six leaf shapes to garnish the centre of the pie dish. Brush the shapes with a little beaten egg before pressing them lightly in place.

8. Make a hole in the middle of the pie using the point of a sharp knife to allow the steam to escape during cooking. Brush the top carefully with beaten egg and chill for 10 minutes in the refrigerator to rest the pastry.

9. Bake the pie for 15 minutes, then reduce the oven temperature to 200°C and bake for a further 15 to 20 minutes, or until the pastry is risen and golden brown. Serve the pie hot with steamed organic vegetables.

Venison Sausages
with Red Cabbage

Serves 4

Ingredients

Venison Sausages 8 to 12 links
Olive Oil 2 tablespoon
Fennel Seeds 1 teaspoon
Red Cabbage 750g, finely shredded
Smoked Chilli Jelly 1 tablespoon
Red Wine Vinegar 1 tablespoon

Belazu Smoked Chilli Jelly is best (from delis and some Sainsbury's Special Selections), although any chilli jelly, or even redcurrant jelly can be used too.

Method

1. Heat the oven to 200°C or 180°C for fan assisted.
2. Bake the sausages in a roasting tin for 30 minutes, turning once.
3. Ten minutes before the sausages are done, heat the oil in a wok over medium heat and add the fennel seeds and red cabbage. Stir fry for 3 minutes, cover and cook for further 3 minutes.
4. Add the chilli jelly and vinegar.
5. Toss it all together until the cabbage is cooked but still has some crunch.
6. Serve with the sausages and any juices.

Braised Duck with Peas

Serves 4

Ingredients

2 Good Quality Ducks, such as Gressingham, each about 1.5 to 2.00kg
200ml Sweet Cider
600ml Basic Gravy
600ml Chicken Stock
Thyme Sprigs
1 Bay Leaf
2 Tablespoons Double Cream
200g Shelled Fresh or Frozen Peas
Sea Salt and Freshly Ground Black Pepper

 Method

1. Preheat the oven to 220°C. Cut the ducks
   in half. Cut off the parson's nose and trim
   away any excess fat and the backbone
   where there isn't any meat. Chop the
   knuckle from the legs and trim the wing
   bones, if necessary. Season the birds with
   salt and pepper, roast them, skin down, in
   a roasting tin for 30 minutes. Transfer the
   ducks to a colander over a bowl to drain
   off the fat.

2. Turn the oven down to 170°C. Carefully
   cut the duck halves into two, where the
   breast joins the leg.

3. Put the duck pieces into a casserole dish
   with the cider, gravy, chicken stock, thyme
   and bay leaf. Cover with a lid and braise for
   1- 4 hours (depending on duck size).
   Remove the ducks from the liquid with a
   slotted spoon, put them on a
   warm plate and cover with foil. Set aside.

4. Transfer the cooking liquid to a saucepan,
   skim off any fat and simmer until reduced
   and thicken. Return the duck to the liquid,
   add the cream and peas just warmed
   through, check the seasoning and serve.

Chicken in
Red Wine

Serves 4

 Ingredients

125g Unsmoked Streaky Bacon, diced and blanched

8 Button Onions, peeled

100g Mushrooms, cut in quarters

75g Butter

1 Oven Ready Chicken (quartered), weighing about 1.5kg

Salt and Freshly Ground Black Pepper

1 Clove Garlic, peeled and crushed

200ml Good Quality Red Burgundy

1 Generous pinch Flour

 Method

1. Fry the bacon, onions and mushroom gently on 50g butter in a flameproof casserole dish until golden brown. Remove the bacon and vegetables and keep warm.

2. Season the chicken, then fry in the same casserole dish until golden brown, add the bacon and vegetables. Cover with a lid and finish cooking in a moderately hot oven (190°C) for about 20 minutes, removing the most tender pieces after a few minutes.

3. Arrange the chicken and garnish in a deep serving dish and keep warm. Remove the fat from the pan and add the garlic and wine. Reduce by half. Mix the remaining butter with a generous pinch of flour and add this to the sauce to thicken it.

4. Pour the sauce over the chicken and serve.

Grilled Skewered Chicken

Serves 4

 Ingredients

8 Chicken Thighs with skin, boned
8 Large Thick Spring Onions (scallions), trimmed
Oil, for greasing
Lemon Wedges, to serve
8 Bamboo skewers

For the Yakitori Sauce
60ml / 4 tablespoons sake
75ml / 5 tablespoons shoyu
15ml / 1 tablespoon mirin
15ml / 1 tablespoon unrefined caster (superfine) sugar or rapadura

 Method

1. Make the Yakitori Sauce. Mix all the ingredients together in a small pan. Bring to the boil, then reduce the heat and simmer for 10 minutes.
2. Cut the chicken into 2.5cm cubes. Cut the spring onions into 2.5 cm long sticks.
3. To cook the chicken on a barbeque, soak the eight bamboo skewers overnight in water. This prevents the skewers from burning during the cooking. Prepare the barbecue. Thread about four pieces of chicken and three spring onion pieces on to each of the skewers. Place the Yakitori sauce in a small bowl and have a brush ready!
4. Cook the skewered chicken on the barbecue. Keep the skewer handles away from the fire, turning them frequently. Brush the chicken with sauce. Return to the coals and repeat this process twice more until

the chicken is well cooked.

5. Alternatively, to grill, preheat the grill to high. Oil the wire rack and spread out the chicken cubes on it. Grill both sides of the chicken until the juices drip, then dip the pieces in the sauce and put back on the rack. Grill for 30 seconds on each side, repeating the dipping process twice more.

6. Set aside and keep warm. Gently grill the spring onions until soft and slightly brown outside. Do not dip. Thread the chicken and spring onion pieces on to skewers as above.

7. Arrange the skewered chicken and spring onions on a serving platter and serve accompanied by lemon wedges.

Derbyshire Trout with Saffron

Serves 2

Ingredients

2 Trout, cleaned
2 Vine tomatoes
Olive Oil
600ml Dry White Wine
1 Pinch of Salt
6 Peppercorns
4 Parsley Stalks
1 Tablespoon Chopped Fresh Fennel

1 Sprig Thyme
1 Bay Leaf
1 Clove of Garlic, crushed
10 Coriander Seeds
1 Large Pinch Saffron Threads

To Garnish
1 Lemon, fluted and sliced
Sprigs of Fennel

Method

1. Put the fish in a well oiled flameproof dish.
2. Peel and core the tomatoes, remove the seeds and chop the tomato flesh roughly. Place this around the trout. Cover with white wine and add all the flavourings.
3. Bring to the boil, cover and place in a moderate oven (180°C). Monitor the oven temperature so as to ensure that the fish simmers very gently for 10 -12 minutes, then remove from the oven and allow the fish to cool fully in the cooking liquid.
4. Serve with a little of the cooking liquid, vegetables and flavourings and garnish with slices of carefully fluted lemon and sprigs of fennel.

Red Onion and Mushroom Tartlets with Goats Cheese

Serves 6

 Ingredients

60ml Olive Oil
25g Butter
4 Red Onions, thinly sliced
1 teaspoon Unrefined Soft Light Brown Sugar
1 tablespoon Balsamic Vinegar
1 tablespoon Soy Sauce
200g Button White Mushrooms, sliced
1 Garlic Clove, finely chopped
1/2 teaspoon Chopped Fresh Tarragon
2 tablespoons Chopped Fresh Parsley

250g Goats Cheese
Sea Salt and Ground Black Pepper
Mixed Salad Leaves, to serve

For the Pastry
200g Plain Flour
Pinch of Cayenne Pepper
90g Butter
40g Freshly Grated Parmesan Cheese
3 to 4 tablespoons Iced Water

 Method

1. To make the pastry, sift the flour and cayenne pepper into a bowl, add the butter and rub in with fingertips.

2. Stir in the parmesan cheese, then bind the pastry with the iced water. Press the pastry into a ball, then wrap it in clear film and chill.

3. Heat 1 tablespoon of the oil and half the butter in a heavy frying pan, then add the onions. Cover and cook gently for 15 minutes, stirring occasionally.

4. Uncover the pan and increase the heat slightly. Sprinkle in the sugar. Cook, stirring frequently until the onions begin to caramelise and brown. Add the balsamic vinegar and soy sauce and heat vigorously

until the liquid evaporates. Season to taste then set aside.

5. Heat another 2 tablespoons of oil and the remaining butter in a pan, add the sliced mushrooms and chopped garlic and cook on high heat for 5 to 6 minutes, or until the mushrooms are browned and cooked.

6. Set a few cooked mushrooms and onion rings aside, then stir the rest of the mushrooms into the onions with the fresh tarragon and parsley. Adjust the seasoning to taste. Preheat the oven to 190°C.

7. Roll out the pastry and use to line six 10cm tartlet tins. Prick the pastry bases with a fork and line the sides with strips of foil. Bake for 10 minutes, remove the foil and

bake for a further 5 to 7 minutes, until the pastry is lightly browned and cooked. Remove from the oven and increase the temperature to 200°C.

8. Remove the pastry shells from the tins and arrange them on a baking sheet. Divide the onion mixture equally among the pastry shells. Cut the goats cheese into six equal slices and place one slice on each tartlet. Distribute the reserved mushrooms and onion rings, drizzle with the remaining oil and season with pepper.

9. Return the tartlets to the oven and bake for 5 to 8 minutes, or until the goats cheese is just beginning to turn brown. Serve with mixed salad leaves.

Spiced Gem Squash

Serves 6 as a starter

 Ingredients

8 Gem Squash
1 Red Pepper, roasted, peeled and finely chopped
1 Yellow Pepper, roasted, peeled and finely chopped
1 Large Onion, chopped

3 Sticks Celery, finely chopped
2 Cloves Garlic
2 Tablespoons Fat Currants

1 Stick Cinnamon

6 Whole Cloves

6 oz Goats Cheese, cut into cubes

2 Tablespoons Parsley

Olive Oil

Salt and Freshly Ground Black Pepper

 Method

1. Preheat the oven to 180°C.

2. Cut six of the squash in half and scoop out the seeds. Cut out the flesh with a grapefruit knife, leaving a thin layer around the tough outer skin.

3. Peel and seed the remaining two squash. Chop all the squash flesh and set aside.

4. Line a baking tray with foil and place the empty halves upside down and place in the oven. Heat through until the flesh softens slightly.

5. Sauté in olive oil, garlic, onion and celery with the cinnamon, cloves and currants.. Once softened, add the diced squash flesh and continue to cook until soft. Season generously and add the diced red and yellow peppers to heat through. Lastly, add the chopped parsley and goat's cheese.

6. Remove the shells from the oven and stuff with the spiced vegetables. Brown under a hot grill and serve immediately with thick, crusty bread.

Summer Vegetable Salad with Goats Cheese

Serves 4

Ingredients

65g Shelled Fresh or Frozen Peas
100g Podded Fresh Young Broad Beans
100g Asparagus Tips
65g Small Salad Leaves
Small Mint Leaves, from 2 or 3 sprigs
75g Soft Goats Cheese, broken into
small pieces
Small Handful of Fine Chives, trimmed

For the Dressing
1 Tablespoon Good Quality White
Wine Vinegar
3 Tablespoons Olive Oil
2 Tablespoons Vegetable Oil
1 Teaspoon Caster Sugar
Few Mint Leaves
Sea Salt and Freshly Ground Black Pepper

Method

1. Cook the vegetables separately in boiling salted water until just tender.
2. To make the dressing, blend the wine vinegar, oils, sugar and mint leaves together in a food processor and season with salt and pepper to taste.
3. Drain the vegetables, refresh in cold water to stop the cooking and drain. Toss the warm drained vegetables with a spoonful or two of the dressing, and season with salt and pepper.
4. Combine the salad leaves and mint leaves in a bowl and lightly dress with some of the dressing. Divide between serving plates, scatter the vegetables on top and spoon over a little more dressing. Arrange the goats cheese on top and finish with the chives.

Baked Apple Dumplings

Serves 8

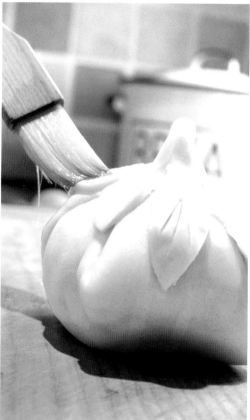

Ingredients
8 Firm Cooking Apples, peeled
1 Egg White
130g Unrefined Caster Sugar
45ml Double Cream or Soya Cream,
plus extra Whipped Cream to Serve
2.5ml Vanilla Essence
250ml Maple Syrup

For the Pastry
475g Plain Flour
350g Butter, diced
175ml Water

Method

1. To make the pastry, sift the flour into a large bowl, rub in the butter until the mixture resembles fine breadcrumbs.

2. Sprinkle over 175ml water and mix until the dough holds together, adding more water if necessary. Gather into a ball. Wrap in clear film and chill for 10 minutes. Preheat oven to 220°C.

3. Cutting from the stem end, core the apples without cutting through the base. Roll out the pastry thinly. Cut squares almost large enough to enclose the apples, brush with egg white, and set an apple in the centre of each.

4. Cut pastry rounds to cover the tops of the cored apples. Reserve the pastry trimmings. Combine the unrefined sugar, cream and vanilla essence in a small bowl. Spoon an eighth of the mixture into the hollow of each apple.

5. Place a pastry round on top of each apple, then bring up the sides of the pastry square to enclose it, pleating the larger piece of pastry to make a snug fit around the apple. Moisten the joins with cold water where they overlap and press down so they stick in place.

6. Make apple stalks and leaves from the pastry trimmings and use to decorate the dumplings. Set them in a large greased baking dish, at least 2cm apart. Bake for 30 minutes, then reduce the oven temperature to 180°C and continue baking for 20 minutes more, or until the pastry is golden brown and the apples are tender.

7. Transfer the dumplings to a serving dish. Mix the maple syrup with the juices in the baking dish and drizzle over the dumplings. Serve the dumplings hot with whipped cream.

Brandied Cherries with Vanilla Ice Cream

Serves 4

 Ingredients

50g Glace Cherries
2 Tablespoons Kirsch
500g Glace à là Vanille,
100g Marrons Glaces (candied chestnuts)
300ml Crème Chantilly

 Method

1. Macerate the glace cherries in the Kirsch for at least half an hour.
2. Place the vanilla ice cream in 4 coupe glasses or bowls and arrange the macerated glace cherries in a group on top of each coupe.
3. Pass the candied chestnuts through a coarse sieve, which will produce a puree that looks rather like vermicelli, and place this on top of the glace cherries. Surround with a decorative border of Crème Chantilly.

The Honey Pot Honey Cheesecake

Ingredients

1¹/₂ Cups Plain Sweet Biscuit Crumbs
¹/₂ Cup Chopped Walnuts
3oz Butter, Melted
3 Cups Creamed Cottage Cheese
¹/₂ Cup Derbyshire Honey
¹/₄ Cup Caster Sugar
4 Eggs
2 Tablespoons Flour
Whipped Cream
Strawberries

Method

1. Combine the biscuit crumbs, chopped walnuts and melted butter. Press firmly over base and sides of a greased 7 inch spring tin.
2. Chill while preparing the mixture.
3. Push the cheese through a sieve and beat in eggs one at a time. Add honey and sugar, beat until smooth.
4. Fold in the flour and turn the mixture onto the crumb crust.
5. Bake in a moderate oven for 1 hour. Leave cheese cake in the oven with the heat turned off and door open until quite cold.
6. To serve, decorate with whipped cream and strawberries.

Poached Pears with Creamed Rice

Serves 6

 Ingredients

6 Small Pears, peeled and cored from the bottom

300ml Vanilla Flavoured Syrup

100g Crystallised ginger, diced

2 Tablespoons Kirsch

100g Short Grain Rice, dry weight, prepared as Riz Pour Entremets (cooked as rice pudding)

$1/2$ Teaspoon Arrowroot

Method

1. Poach the pears in the syrup and drain, reserving the syrup.
2. Soak the crystallised ginger in half of the kirsch and add most of these to the prepared rice, reserving a few for decoration.
3. Arrange a border of this rice round a serving dish and arrange the poached pears in the centre. Decorate with the reserved crystallised ginger.
4. Reduce the reserved pear syrup, thicken with a little arrowroot and flavour with the remaining kirsch. Pour over the top of the pears.

Strawberry Sundae

Crème Frangipane

Ingredients

750ml Milk
1 Vanilla Pod
100g Sugar
100g Flour
2 Eggs
4 Egg Yolks
Pinch of Salt
75g Butter
25g Crushed Macaroons

Method

Boil the milk and infuse with the vanilla for 30 minutes. Place the sugar, flour, eggs, egg yolks and salt in a pan and stir with a wooden spoon. Slowly stir in the hot milk and bring to the boil gently, stirring continuously. Allow to boil for 2 minutes then transfer to a bowl. Add 50g of the butter and the crushed macaroons, stir well. Smooth the surface with the remaining butter on the point of a knife to prevent a skin from forming.

Makes 750ml

Crème Chantilly

Ingredients

500ml Double Cream
65g Caster Sugar
1/2 teaspoon Vanilla Essence

Method

Whisk the cream until it becomes stiff enough to stand in peaks on the whisk. Add the sugar and vanilla essence : mix well. This cream should be prepared at the last moment.

Makes 500ml

Crème à l'Anglaise

Ingredients

200g Caster Sugar
6 Egg Yolks
1/2 teaspoon Arrowroot
600ml Boiling Milk

Method

Place the sugar, arrowroot and egg yolks in a basin and whisk until the mixture thickens and forms a dissolving ribbon when the whisk is lifted out of the basin.

Add the boiled milk, slowly, a little at a time, place over the heat and stir with a wooden spoon until the yolks thicken the mixture and it sticks to the back of the spoon. Do not boil the custard, as this will cause it to separate. When cooked, pass the custard through a fine strainer and keep warm in a bain-marie. When used as a sauce, this egg custard can be flavoured as desired. For example, use vanilla, orange or lemon zest infused in the milk, or 50ml of your favourite liqueur.

Makes 600ml

White Chocolate Mousse Torte

Serves 12

 Ingredients

For the Biscuit Base
200g Amaretti Biscuits
100g Unsalted Butter, melted

For the Mousse
350g White Chocolate
500ml Double Cream, at room temperature
4 Tablespoon Milk, at room temperature

 Method

1. Crush the amaretti biscuits in a food processor until they look like fine crumbs, transfer to a bowl and mix in the melted butter. Tip the mixture into the prepared cake tin and press firmly over the base with the back of a spoon.

2. Break the chocolate into pieces and melt in a heatproof bowl, set over a saucepan of simmering water. Set aside and let cool until lukewarm.

3. Put the cream and milk in a bowl and using an electric hand held mixer, whisk until the mixture leaves a ribbon-like trail on the surface when the mixer is lifted out of the bowl.

4. Using a large metal spoon, stir a spoonful of the whipped cream mixture into the chocolate to slacken, then immediately put it into the remaining cream mixture. Stir vigorously until smooth and mousse-like. Don't worry if there are tiny lumps of chocolate flecked in the mixture - it will taste delicious.

5. Pour into the prepared tin and whirl the top. Cover and refrigerate for at least 4 hours or overnight. When set, remove the tin, but leave the base on and peel off the paper collar. Let stand for a few minutes to soften, then cut into thin slices and serve.

Bloomers Original Bakewell Pudding Recipe

Serves 6

Ingredients

6 to 8oz Puff Paste 'Pastry'
4 to 6oz Sieved Strawberry Jam
4oz Caster Sugar
6 Eggs
3oz Unsalted Butter
4oz Ground Almonds

 Method

1. Roll out the pastry, line the shallow pie dish, prick the base.
2. Cover the base with the jam.
3. Melt the butter.
4. Separate the eggs, use only the yolks.
5. Beat together all the ingredients; pour in

Derbyshire Honey and Lemon Curd

 Ingredients

4 Lemons
4oz Butter
454g Clear Derbyshire Honey
4 Eggs

 Method

1. Grate lemon rinds and squeeze and strain juice.
2. Put into double saucepan with butter and honey.
3. Beat the eggs and egg yokes, strain them into the mixture, cook and stir over a gentle heat until thick and creamy.
4. Pour into hot jars and cover.

Note: This will keep for 2 months.

Derbyshire Honey Fruit Cake

Serves 12

Ingredients

227g/ 8oz self-raising flour
113g/ 4oz butter
56g/ 2oz peel
113g/ 4oz sultanas
227g/ 8oz Derbyshire Clear Honey
113g/ 4oz currents
2 eggs
Pinch of nutmeg and salt
3 tablespoons of milk

 Method

1. Cream honey and butter together.

2. Beat eggs well and add alternately with sifted flour, nutmeg and salt. Add fruit, peel

Strawberry Jam
and Scones

Ingredients

For the Strawberry Jam
1 kg Small Strawberries
900g Unrefined Granulated Sugar
Juice of 2 Lemons

For the Scones
225g Plain Flour
15 ml Baking Powder
50g Butter
1 Egg Beaten
75 ml Milk
Clotted or double cream

Method

1. Layer the strawberries and sugar in a large bowl. Cover and leave overnight.

2. The next day, tip the strawberries and their juices into a large heavy pan. Add the lemon juice. Bring to the boil, stirring until the sugar has dissolved.

3. Boil steadily for 10 - 15 minutes. Spoon a small amount on to a chilled saucer. Chill for 3 minutes, then push the jam with your finger, if wrinkles form, it is ready. Cool for 10 minutes.

4. Pour the strawberry jam into warm sterilized jars, filling them right to the top. Cover the jam with a disc of waxed paper and seal the jar with a damp cellophane round and secure with an elastic band while the jam is still hot. Label and store in a dark place.

5. To make the scones, preheat the oven to 220°C. Butter a baking sheet. Sift the flour and baking powder together, then rub in the butter or margarine. Make a well in the centre of the flour mixture, add the egg and milk and mix to a soft dough, using fork or a round bladed knife.

6. Turn out the scone dough on to a floured surface, and kneed very lightly until smooth. Roll out the dough to about 2 cm thickness and cut into 10 or 12 rounds using a cutter.

7. Transfer to the baking sheet, brush the tops with egg, then bake for about 8 minutes, until risen and golden. Cool slightly on a wire rack then serve with the jam and clotted or double cream.

Barry Garton
at Bournes Restaurant, Denby Pottery

Nut and Red Wine Pate

Serves 4 - 6

A recipe from the newly refurbished Bourne's Restaurant at Denby Visitor Centre

Earlier this year, the restaurant at Denby Visitor Centre underwent a complete refurbishment. Now called 'Bourne's' after the family who owned and ran Denby for many years, the restaurant has a new coffee area and an extended menu with a distinct Derbyshire flavour. There's new choices for children's, a Derbyshire dish of the day, delicious homemade cakes, salad bar and Denby's own blend of coffee.

Manager of Bourne's Barry Garton has selected the delicious recipe opposite from his new menu.

Also at Denby Visitor Centre you can now buy locally produced foods in the Food section of the Cookery Emporium. There's flour, cheese, meats, cakes, oils, herbs, pates and teas as well as seasonal specials. Select the best from a huge range of kitchen equipment and you can even watch a free demonstration in the kitchen theatre at 12.30 and 2.30 every day and pick up a recipe.

Ingredients

2 small onions

1 clove garlic (optional)

3 medium eggs

3 celery sticks

$1/2$ oz of butter or margarine

1 tsp ground cumin

1 tsp paprika

1 tsp basil

$1/4$ pint water

$1/4$ - $1/2$ pint of red wine (depending upon taste)

1 tbsp soy sauce

5 oz walnuts

5 oz ground almonds

5 oz almond nibs

3 oz breadcrumbs (white or brown)

Salt and pepper to taste

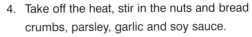

 Method

1. Pre-head the oven to 180°C (350°F/gas mark 4).

2. Grease and line the base and sides of a 2lb loaf tin.

3. Melt the butter in a pan, meanwhile, finely chop the onion and celery. Sauté the vegetables until soft, add the spices and herbs and cook for a further minute, then add the water and wine and bring to the boil.

4. Take off the heat, stir in the nuts and bread crumbs, parsley, garlic and soy sauce.

5. Mix well, add the beaten eggs and season generously.

6. Spoon the mixture into the prepared tin and bake for about 45 minutes until slightly firm to the touch.

Leave to cool down, then turn on to a plate. Slice and serve.

Rachel Green
The Flying Chef

Roasted Fennel, Chicory and Orange Pepper Salad

Serves 4 - 6

 Ingredients

2 bulbs of fennel, outer leaves removed.
1 large orange pepper, cored, seeds and membrane removed
2 head of chicory
grate rind of an orange and its juice
3 sprigs of thyme
2 bay leaves
1 clove garlic sliced
olive oil
1 tablespoon balsamic vinegar
Salt and pepper

 Method

Pre-heat oven to 190°C or gas mark 6.

1. Cut each fennel into 6. Cut the peppers into 6 and cut the chicory into half lengthways.
2. Place the vegetables on a baking sheet with the bay leaves, garlic, orange rind and sprigs of thyme. Drizzle a generous amount of olive oil over the top and season with sea salt and black pepper.
3. Roast in the oven for 10 minutes.
4. Remove from the oven and drizzle with balsamic vinegar, the juice of the orange and the cooking juices.

Serve with griddled chicken.

Pan Fried Derbyshire Chicken Breasts with Pine Nuts & Cherry Tomatoes

Serves 4

Scott Brown at
Brownies Restaurant,
The Three Horseshoes,
Wessington

 Ingredients

4 Derbyshire Chicken Supremes (bone in & skin on)
4oz Pine Nuts
Bunch of Basil
8oz Cherry Tomatoes
Balsamic Vinegar reduced by half with Brown Sugar to your taste
Coarse Rock Salt and Black Pepper
Light Leaf Salad to garnish

 Method

1. With a very thin film of olive oil in a hot frying pan (preferably oven proof), place the chicken supremes skin side down and seal until slightly browned.
2. Turn over and seal the other side. Sprinkle the skin with coarse rock salt and black pepper.
3. Transfer to medium to high oven gas mark 5-6 for 10-15 minutes depending on the size of the supreme. When the chicken is near to being fully cooked, add the tomatoes and pine nuts to the pan and replace in the oven to finish - approximately 5 minutes.
4. Prepare a light leaf salad on the plates. Rip up the basil and divide equally among the plates. Take the pan with the chicken, tomatoes and pine nuts from the oven and allow to rest for 3-5 minutes. Place the chicken on the basil and leaf salad. Spoon over equal quantities of tomatoes and pine nuts, drizzle with balsamic vinegar and dress with herbs and serve.

Paul Morley
at Carsington Water's
Main Sail Restaurant

Fillet of Salmon, with Herb Mash and a Garlic & Chilli Butter Serves 4

 Ingredients

4 x 6oz Salmon fillets
8oz Butter
1 Green chilli, finely chopped
1 Red chilli, finely chopped
2 Cloves of Garlic
1 Tablespoon of Fresh Parsley
1 Tablespoon of Fresh Chives
3 Tablespoons of Sunflower or Olive Oil
Ground Black Pepper & Salt
2lb of Peeled potatoes (diced)

 Method

1. Boil the potatoes for 15 - 20 minutes until cooked. Whilst the potatoes are cooking, heat a frying pan with the Sunflower or Olive Oil.

2. Season the salmon with a pinch of salt and pepper and place in a pan skin side down for 2 minutes, place in a baking tray in an oven (170°C) for 5 - 10 minutes.

3. Drain the potatoes, put back in the pan and return to the heat to dry. Season with a pinch of salt and pepper.

4. Add 2oz of butter and the chives then stir through.

5. Melt the remaining 6oz of butter in the pan then leave to rest for 5 minutes. Slowly pour into a bowl leaving the sediment behind, add the finely chopped chillies, parsley and garlic.

6. Season with salt and freshly ground black pepper to taste.

7. Assembly
   Place the mashed potato in the centre of the plate, top with the salmon and drizzle with the garlic and chilli butter.
   Garnish with a lemon and fresh parsley.

Paul Morley

As a qualified chef, Paul Morley has completed courses in Kitchen and Larder, Hospitality and Catering and worked in hotels and venues around Derbyshire. With the aspiration to be a chef Paul started his career at the East Lodge Hotel and the following years would see him travel across the world.

Having toured and worked his way through Australia at successful restaurants in Perth, Darwin and Cairns as chef and head chef and sampling such pursuits as sky diving, bungee jumping and white water rafting Paul came back to Britain with a fresh, vibrant approach to cooking and a desire for a challenge.

This experience added to his drive to create freshly cooked, interesting dishes and building on his existing skills, Paul was able to bring this wealth of experience to Carsington Water's Main Sail Restaurant as head chef, a position he has held since 2004.

His distinctive style, using local ingredients wherever possible, combined with outstanding service and fantastic views has created a restaurant celebrated in the local area. With wider recognition coming from Peak District Cuisine and the UK Wedding Day Venue Association the Main Sail Restaurant and Carsington Water have emerged as one of Derbyshire's great restaurants and hospitality venues.

Staff at Carsington Water are 'absolutely delighted' after the centre received a four-star rating for its wedding services.

The Visitor Centre attraction is the first public site in the country to receive such a high rating from the UK Wedding Day Venue Association, meaning it now ranks alongside top hotels. The award came after staff applied for accreditation from the association, which sent officers out to check the quality of service on offer.

Inspectors spoke to couples who had already tied the knot at the venue, had a meal prepared for them by Carsington Water caterers New Leaf and called 'on spec' to see the service for themselves before making their decision. As a result the venue received four stars for its standards of excellence, the highest possible is five.

Ken Leach, chief of classification for the association, visited Carsington Water recently to present staff with a certificate marking their achievement.

Pictured with the award are (l-r) Visitor Marketing Manager John Concannon, Ken Leach, of the UK Wedding Venue Association, Hospitality Manager Pam Fletcher, and Mike Tempest, Manager of New Leaf Catering.

Wayne Rogers
at The Nettle Inn, Mill Town, Ashover
Potted Ham Hock with Pork Scratchings
Serves 4

Ingredients

For the Ham Hock
2 Ham Hocks
1 Onion
2 Bay leafs
5g Mixed Peppercorns
10g Gherkin's (chopped)
10g Capers (whole)
15g Parsley
Grain Mustard
20g Butter
Crack Black Pepper

For the Chutney
2 Apples
Sage
2 tablespoon Cider Vinegar
Sultanas
1/2 Onion
50ml Granulated Sugar
5ml Ground Cinnamon

Bacon Fat
Salt
Butter
4 x crusts of Homemade Bread

Scratching
Rub Fat with butter and salt
Pre Heat oven to 220°C
Slice into 2 inch strips, place in oven, cook for about 20 mins

 Method

1. Put hocks, onion, bay leaves and mixed peppercorns into a pan and cook in cold water, bring to the boil and skim off any scum on the top
2. Cook for about 3 to 4 hours, till the meat is falling of the bone. Leave to cool in the liquor.
3. Take the hocks out, put in a bowl and add capers, gherkins, parsley, mustard and pepper.
4. Meanwhile pass the liquor and reduce by 1/4 till it is 1/3 and add into the bowl.
5. Melt butter, put the hock mixture into keilner jars and pour melted butter over until it covers the contents.
6. Place in the fridge until needed

Chutney
1. Peel and core the apples, peel and quarter the onion and cut both into about 1cm squares, put in a pan along with the vinegar.
2. Slowly bring to the boil. Reduce the heat and simmer for 30 minutes.
3. Add the sultanas and sugar and cook until chutney is thick, but don't let it catch on the bottom of the pan.
4. Add the cinnamon and chopped sage and place in a sterilized jar. Ideally leave for about 1 month before using.

Jason Wardill
at The White Bear, Stretton

Roast Breast of Derbyshire Chicken, Green Olives and Coriander, Cumin and Orange Baby Carrots, and Parmentier Potatoes Serves 4

 Ingredients

4 Skin on Chicken Breasts
2 Large Red Potatoes, peeled & diced into neat cubes as in the picture
1 Bunch of Baby Carrots, peeled & washed
1 Cup of Fresh Orange Juice
1 Teaspoon of Ground Cumin
Olive Oil
50g Minced Ginger
50g Minced Onion
Pinch of Saffron Strands or Ground Turmeric
450ml Good Strong Chicken Stock
2 Tablespoons of Minced Green Olives
2 Tablespoons of Lemon Juice
1 Heaped Tablespoon of Coarsely Chopped Coriander
1 Stick of Cinnamon
Sunflower Oil
Salt & Pepper

Method

1. To cook the potatoes place them in a pan and cover with cold water add a little salt and bring to the boil and cook until potatoes become tender, refresh them in cold water to stop the cooking process. Take care not to overcook the potatoes as they will lose their cube shape when you come to fry them later. Once cooled, place them on a paper towel in the fridge until you need them.

2. To cook the carrots, place the peeled and washed carrots in a pan and cover with the orange juice and a little water, add a little salt and the cumin. Cook the carrots until just tender, then take off the heat and allow to cool in the liquid. Set to one side until the dish is ready to serve.

3. For the olives and coriander, fry the ginger and onions gently over a medium heat then add the saffron or turmeric and the cinnamon, a pinch of salt and cook for a further 5 minutes. Next add the chicken stock and turn up to a high heat to reduce the stock by so the mixture will be thick and syrupy, set the sauce to one side.

To Serve the Dish

4. Place a pan on heat and make sure it is nice and hot, then add a little sunflower oil. Season the chicken breasts with salt and pepper, then sear the skin side down until golden brown. Turn over and colour the other side. Turn the breasts back onto the skin side and then place the pan in a hot oven and cook the breasts for around 15 - 20 minutes or until cooked through.

5. At this stage you can add a spoonful of olive oil to the reduced stock mix and the minced olives, coriander and a squeeze of lemon juice. Check the mix for salt and pepper and adjust to your liking.

6. Warm the carrots up in the cooking liquid, meanwhile in a non-stick pan, fry the cooked cubes of potato in hot oil until golden on all sides (at the restaurant we fry the potatoes in duck fat which gives them a great flavour) and then season well with salt and pepper.

7. Sit the rested roast breast of chicken in the centre of a warm plate, arrange the potatoes around the edge and the warmed carrots as in the photo. Finally, spoon around the olive oil and coriander mixture. You can garnish the dish with a little mustard cress or some soft herbs.

" This is a dish I really enjoy eating as it's refreshing and light and the flavours work so well together. It is a little bit of work but well worth the effort both to look at and to eat. I hope you will give it a go and entertain your friends with something a little different. **"**

Mr Rahman
at Jeera, Codnor, Derbyshire

Chicken Jalali - Award winning curry
Serves 4

Rave reviews for its fine Indian cuisine has put Codnor's Jeera on the map. The surroundings are smart & stylish with low key lighting creating a warm & relaxed atmosphere that is perfect for a candle lit meal. Courteous staff, comfortable seating & generous portions of the most delicious Indian cuisine produced by an award-winning chef make a trip to Jeera well worth it.

Ingredients

6 Chicken Breasts, diced
2 Tins of Chopped Tomatoes
2 Onions, finely chopped
4 teaspoon Curry Powder
2 teaspoon Chilli Powder
16 Cayenne Chillies, de-seeded & sliced lengthways
Head of Garlic
4" Root Ginger, grated

5 tablespoon Vegetable Oil
2 Handfuls Coriander Leaves, finely chopped
1 Handful Coriander Leaves, whole (garnish)
2 teaspoon Garam Masala
1 tablespoon Cumin Seeds
8 Cardamom Seeds
2 Green Peppers, chopped
Yoghurt
Mint

Method

1. Make a paste of the curry & chilli powders with a little water.
2. Heat the frying pan, pour in the oil & fry the onions until translucent.
3. Add the cardamom & cumin seeds, garlic, ginger, chilli, garam masala & green peppers and stir fry on medium for a few minutes.

4. Add the curry & chilli powder paste, yoghurt & mint, stir in and fry for 30 seconds.
5. Add the chicken and seal on all sides.
6. Add the tomatoes & simmer for 20 minutes or until chicken is cooked, stirring frequently. If needed, add more water to stop the curry becoming too thick or dry.
7. Add the finely chopped coriander leaves, cook for a further minute.

Serve with whole coriander leaves sprinkled over the top with rice and / or naan bread.

Richard Young
of the Original Farmers' Market Shop, Bakewell

Three Bird Roast Serves 6 - 8

 Ingredients

The three birds to be used are:

1 Duck

1 Chicken

1 Pheasant.

Bacon

Sausage Meat

Stuffing Mix

Red Currant Jelly

   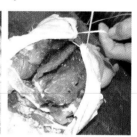

 Method

1. Bone the duck
2. Remove the chicken fillets
3. Remove the pheasant fillets
4. Layer the duck with the sausage meat
5. Layer with bacon
6. Add stuffing mix
7. Place chicken fillets in stuffing mix
8. Add more sausage meat
9. Add more bacon to cover the chicken fillets and sausage meat, top with the pheasant fillets
10. Re-assemble
11. Spread red currant jelly over the pheasant fillets

12. Sew duck back together, tie off the string, sprinkle with herbs
13. Roast the finished 3 bird roast as per chicken and use a meat thermometer to ensure the bird is cooked through.

Scott Heath

at the Saracen's Head, Shirley

White Chocolate & Coconut Cheesecake

Serves 4

Ingredients
100g Cream Cheese
4 Large Organic Eggs, separated
1/2 pt Whipping Cream
140g Caster Sugar
125g White Chocolate
10g Gelatine
1 Coconut
10 Chocolate Hobnob Biscuits,
crushed
75g Butter
50g Dark Chocolate
2xA4 Sheets Acetate

Method

For The Base

Melt the butter in a pan and stir in the crushed hobnobs. Divide the biscuit base into the 4 mould rings and press down. Place in the fridge to set.

For The Cheesecake Mix

Whip together the sugar, egg yolks, cream cheese & coconut milk until smooth. Melt the white chocolate over a pan of warm water & add the gelatine, mixing to ensure the chocolate doesn't set. When fully mixed to a smooth consistency, introduce 1 spoon each of the whipped cream & whipped egg white before adding the remaining eggs and cream. This ensures a light & creamy texture. Pour the mixture evenly onto each base & return to the fridge for approximately 1 hour or until set.

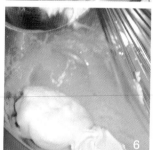

For The Cage

You will need 2 A4 sheets of acetate, cut lengthways. Lay the 4 strips on a flat surface. Melt the dark chocolate over a pan of warm water & pipe the chocolate over the acetate in a kriss-cross pattern. With the remaining chocolate, pipe out 4 lids. Remove the cheesecakes from the rings & wrap the acetate strips around the outside. Return to the fridge for approximately 10 minutes to allow the chocolate to set. When set, carefully remove the acetate strip, producing the chocolate cage. Place the lid on top & garnish with coconut shavings & seasonal berries.

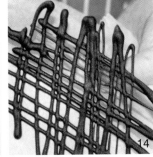

AGA
recipes

Eastern Fish Brochettes

Serves 6 as a starter

 Ingredients

675g Monkfish

For the Marinade
1 Large Onion, finely chopped
1 Clove of Garlic, crushed
1 tablespoon Fresh Coriander, finely chopped
2 tablespoon Fresh Parsley, finely chopped
1 teaspoon Saffron
1 teaspoon Hot Pepper Sauce
6 tablespoon Olive Oil
6 tablespoon Lime Juice
Salt & Freshly Ground Black Pepper

For the Relish
150ml Yoghurt
2 tablespoon Fresh Mint, finely chopped
1 teaspoon Caster Sugar
A Little Milk

To Garnish
Lime Wedges
Fresh Coriander
6 Metal Skewers

 Method

1. Cut the fish into 2.5cm (1 inch) cubes and slide onto metal skewers - soak for an hour in cold water before use.
2. Mix the marinade ingredients together.
3. Place the brochettes in a shallow container that will just hold them, and spoon over the marinade. Leave in the fridge for 2-3 hours.
4. To make the relish, mix the yoghurt, mint and sugar together. Add just enough milk to thin to a pouring consistency. Chill until ready to use.
5. 2,3 & 4 oven Aga
   Line a roasting tin with Bake-O-Glide and place a grill rack in the high position. Add the brochettes and slide the tin onto the highest set of runners in the roasting oven. Grill for 5-10 minutes, turning twice. Cook until the fish is very lightly browned.
6. Garnish with lime wedges and coriander. Serve the relish separately.
7. Conventional Cooking
   Cook under a pre-heated grill at a medium to high setting.

Tipsy Cake Serves 8

Ingredients
200g Divine (Dark) Chocolate
175g Softened Butter
175g Golden Caster Sugar
3 Eggs
175g Self Raising Flour
1 Level teaspoon Baking Powder
1 Orange
75g White Chocolate, chopped

For the Syrup
100g Granulated Sugar
3-4 tablespoon Cointreau or other orange liqueur

To Complete
142ml Double Cream
4 tablespoon Single Cream
A 23cm/9" Springform Cake Tin, Lightly Greased and Base Lined with Bake-O-Glide

Method
1. Break half the chocolate into a bowl; melt then cool; reserve remainder for the top.
2. Cream the butter and sugar together, slowly add the beaten eggs with a little flour then fold in all the dry ingredients with the finely grated orange rind. If the mixture is too stiff, add a little orange juice.
3. Spoon half the mixture into a bowl with the melted chocolate & stir the white chocolate into the other half.
4. Space spoons of the white mixture in the tin with the chocolate in between and gently smooth over the top.
5. Bake towards the bottom half of the baking oven for about 35 minutes until cooked through, covering if necessary. For the 2 oven Aga, bake on the grid shelf on the lowest lug with the cold shelf immediately above it; watch the timing. Cool a little in the tin before turning out.
6. Return the cake to the clean tin. Dissolve the sugar in 4 tablespoons of water. When the sugar granules have disappeared, bring the syrup to boil for 3 or 4 minutes until slightly thicker, add any orange juice. Cool before adding the liqueur then pour over the cake in the tin. Later, lift the cake onto a pretty plate.
7. Either melt the reserved chocolate and make chocolate decorations, or grate it. Lightly whip the creams together then swirl it over the top of the marble cake and decorate with chocolate.
8. For conventional ovens, bake in a moderately hot oven 190°C , 375°F, Gas Mark 5 for about 35 minutes until cooked in the centre.

taste derbyshire -
places to dine

Food looks so much better on fine tableware

Tastes and fashions may change but the decorative and artistic skills that make our wares stand out are as popular today as they have ever been.

Renowned for 250 years for the manufacture of lightly potted and exquisitely decorated porcelain and bone china, Royal Crown Derby is synonymous with superlative quality and distinctive productions - including tableware, giftware and the paperweights and miniatures that are highly collectable today.

Royal Crown Derby

To view the range
call at our showroom on
Osmaston Road, Derby
or visit our web site
www.royalcrownderby.co.uk

fruit&vegwholesale

Telephone: *3am-10am* 01332 363663 or 01332 380612
Mobile: 07968 736159   Fax: 01332 382383
Email: info@mandbfruits.co.uk

Large Enough to Cope
Small Enough to Care

A valued customer with
an array of our produce

The Cock Inn

at Muggington DE6 4PJ

Tel: 01773 550293 Fax: 01773 550867

Come and find our stall at Bolsover Castle.
Lots of gifts with a taste of Wine
Award winning establishment.
Country Inn with breathtaking views overlooking
the Kedleston Estate and Burton Valley.

Evening Specials
Monday - Curry rice and chips £3.95
Tuesday - Roast 'n' Yorkshire Pudding £3.95
Wednesday - Mercaston Sausage and Mash £3.95
Thursday - Sizzling Steaks from £4.95
Friday - Fish extravaganza from £6.95
Sunday - Always get the most from your roast form £4.25

We look forward to seeing you - Book your table now

The
Saracens Head

Home-made Food • Fine Ales
Warm Welcome

Food served 12-2.30, 6.30-9pm
Closed Tuesday.
Open all day Sunday

Tel: 01335 360330
Shirley, Ashbourne, Derbyshire DE6 3AS

HOMESFORD COTTAGE INN

Whatstandwell, Matlock.

01629 822342

English and Mediterranean cuisine including pasta, steak dishes, seafood. Mexican and Greek. All food freshly cooked. Traditional Sunday Roast. Bar snacks always available.

Carsington Water

The Main Sail Restaurant
Carsington Water, Nr Ashbourne

Open all Year

Fabulous restaurant with stunning views
Award winning food
Friendly and efficient service

Outdoor entertaining including hog roast and barbeque
Licensed for civil wedding ceremonies
Marquee wedding receptions

New Leaf

For further information please call
01629 540363
New Leaf Catering, Carsington Water
Ashbourne, Derbyshire DE6 1ST

The Sanam
Tandoori Restaurant

Authentic Indian food served in a lively warm and friendly atmosphere

Take-Away Hotline
01773 830690

FREE delivery on orders over £15.00 within 5 miles radius

50 King Street,
Alfreton. Telephone 01773 830690
Opening Times Sunday to Thursday 6.00pm to 12.00am
Friday & Saturday 6.00pm to 1.00am

EUROCARD
MasterCard
VISA
DELTA

Bourne's
RESTAURANT

New Bourne's

The newly refurbished Restaurant at Denby
Visitor Centre is open daily 9.30am – 4.30pm

• New coffee area • All day snacks
• Lunches 12-3pm • Sunday Carvery
• New menu • Choice of seating areas

Denby

Visitor Centre
Call: 01773 740799

OPEN DAILY. Off A38 on B6179, 2 miles south of Ripley

Finest foods
from the County

Traditional 'Free-Range' Butchers Shop Now Open in Brailsford

- Home bred and reared Highland Beef
- Free range rare breed Lamb
- Free range rare breed Pork
- Free range Poultry and Barbary Duck
- Traditional Bacon
- Speciality Sausages

Find our Shop at:
The Mercaston Food Company,
Express Courtyard, Luke Lane,
Brailsford, Derbyshire.

Open Monday to Saturday from 8.30am

Telephone: 01335 361400   www.mercastonfood.com

Get more from taste derbyshire on line at www.tastederbyshire.co.uk

Robin Maycock

HOLLOWAY VILLAGE BUTCHER

Derbyshire's Premier Butchers Shop.

All our meat is selected from Derbyshire and Nottinghamshire farmers by me personally, transported by me and slaughtered in our own licensed premises behind the shop.

If you care about Quality meat, Service and Welfare and you enjoy eating meat, give us a visit (No yellow lines) or telephone us and ask for Robin. We also deliver free of charge. HOME-MADE. (At the back of the shop) Ham, Ox tongue, Haslet, Roast Pork, Turkey, Salt beef.

HOME COOKED (In our own bakery by Glynis and staff) Steak and kidney pies, steak and onion pies, Quiche, Chicken and mushroom pies, Cornish pasties, Sausage rolls, Cheese and Onion pies, Bakewell tarts, Coconut tarts, Apple Pies (with real Bramley Apples), Blackberry and Apple Pies, Mince Meat and Apple Pie, Lemon Meringues, Custards, Fruit Cakes, Chocolate Cakes, Lemon Cakes, Bread and Butter Puddings, Pizzas, Scotch Eggs, Pork Pies.

English and Continental Cheese, Fresh Fruit and Vegetables

New Lines just introduced - Sticky Toffee Puddings

Ready meals (at a price you can afford) Liver and Onion, Lasagne, Chilli, Chicken a la King, Braising Steak in Gravy, Vegetable Lasagne, Fish Pie, Lamb Curry, Sweet and Sour Pork, Home-Made Sausage (Fresh daily) Pork and Chive, Pork and Herb, Cumberland, Pork and Tomato, Plain Pork.

Bring your own dish and let us make a real Home-Made pie for that special occasion. Pie and Pea Supper a speciality

If you care about food as much as we do give us a ring on
01629 534333 and Ask for Robin or Glynis.

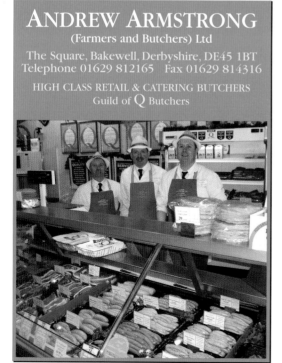

More tasty places to dine in Derbyshire

Canal Inn
Bullbridge

The Nettle Inn
Ashover

Brownies
Wessington

There are some places that just convey that homely, comfortable feel and the Canal Inn at Bullbridge is just like going home and putting on your most comfortable pair of slippers.

David & Lorraine have now run the Canal successfully for the last few years and while still maintaining a true pub feel, they have reflected this in their menu of traditional English food to eat in or take-away.

As people don't all have the same size appetite for their roast dinner, they offer both a smaller size and a very generous size portion. But their menu has seen a comprehensive overhaul with the addition of many new dishes and, after an extremely busy day at work, dining at The Canal, rather than go home and cook, is an excellent option.

Sundays are quite unique, with lunch being served from 12 noon to 8pm! Another unique service is an eleven pitch caravan park, all with electric hook-ups.

Canal Inn,
Bullbridge Hill, Bullbridge.
01773 852739
Open - Monday to Thursday
6pm to 9pm.
Friday and Saturday 6pm to 9.30pm.
Sunday 12noon to 8pm.

The Nettle Inn has long been popular, with its real log fires and comfortable interior. It seems to have combined the relaxed atmosphere of an Inn with a very separate and pleasantly decorated restaurant. Situated just at the junction between Ashover and Milltown, it is just a pretty 10 mins drive off the main Chesterfield/Derby Road.

The owner, Sanford, and his chef have tried to produce a menu that really does cater for all tastes.

The bar menu has some traditional English dishes, while the specials boards, as well as offering dishes we are quite familiar with, also offers the more unusual and very seasonal dishes, with a selection of the best of world cuisine.

If you just fancy sitting by the log fire, enjoying a drink, then the Nettle boasts finely kept ales along with a very reasonably priced wine menu.

The Nettle Inn, Ashover.
01246 590462
Opening Hours: Mon-Sat 12-3.00
and 5.30 to close.
All day Sunday
Lunch and bar snacks, steakboard
and specials.

Good food can be judged by the time it takes to prepare and the attention to detail that is applied when plating up. Scott Brown, the proprietor and chef at Brownies restaurant is a master at both, no detail is overlooked in his preparation of the fine food he serves.

Many restaurants make the mistake of having too many dishes on offer on their menu, thus creating the problem of the chefs not being able to give each dish its just amount of time to create that memorable meal.

That doesn't happen at Brownies, Scott has a well balanced menu which benefits from the use of local ingredients. His attention to detail recently enabled him to win the prestigious 2005 Peak District Cuisine competition awarded by the University of Derby College for the over 25's.

The Three Horseshoes,
Wessington.
01773 834854
Open. Restaurant Friday - Saturday
7pm - 9pm
Bar Meals:
Tuesday - Saturday 12am - 2pm
Tuesday - Thursday
5.30pm - 8.30pm
Sunday 12.30am - 5pm

The Yew Tree
South Wingfield

On the periphery of the old village of South Wingfield is The Yew Tree Pub, owned by Phil and Dave. You cannot help but be drawn by the welcoming lights in the cottage style windows of this village inn

The menu provides a variety of dishes from traditional Thai cooking to authentic French, and a selection of grills.

During the week, at lunch time and early evening, they offer a special menu. Their evening a la carte menu is extensive. The menu changes rapidly so even if you eat there frequently there is always something new to try.

The blazing fire, which on winter evenings pulls like a magnet is a treat to sit by and enjoy a coffee or one of the fine beers on offer.

The Yew Tree Inn, Manor Road, South Wingfield.
01773 833763
Early Doors Menu - Last orders 6.30pm, Mon-Fri.
Two Course Lunch - Tuesday - Saturday 12 until 2pm
A La carte menu 5pm -9pm Monday - Saturday
Sunday lunch 12noon onwards.

Valentino's
Ripley

Although Ripley is a bustling market town by day, it does not immediately spring to mind as a place to visit on a Saturday evening for a meal out. So when we were invited by friends to dine at Valentino's Mediterranean Restaurant, I looked forward to the experience with interest.

Valentino's is just off the market place in Ripley, so parking is both convenient and free. The atmosphere is cosy, lively and friendly with a medley of modern music playing in the background.

This is definitely a Mediterranean restaurant, with authentic dishes sourced from Italy, Mexico, France and Greece. Dishes such as Salmon St Tropez, mixed meze, medallions of beef, chicken breast stuffed with cheese covered in a tequila and chilli sauce, Baileys chocolate fudge sundae, with lashings of Baileys liqueur poured over fresh cream which topped the hot chocolate fudge cake covered in custard, are just a smattering of the array of dishes on offer.

Valentino's Mediterranean Restaurant.
6 High Street, Ripley.
01773 512244

Anoki Restaurant
Derby

Fresh petals and tea lights edge the staircase as you enter Anoki Restaurant, owned by Naveed, who exudes a passion and love for his restaurant. Since opening, Anoki has become a firm favourite for diners.

The restaurant has a high domed ceiling with decorative plaster work, picked out in gold, pinks and blues, on the wall are huge canvasses of a beautiful Indian girl. The high back chairs create their own privacy. The waiters are dressed in the traditional Indian style - a ruby red embroidered tunic and white turban, with pleated fan and long white tail.

The variety of food includes: chargrilled chicken, - creamy cod with prawns in a spicy batter, little discs of tamarind pastry with a coulis dip, - soft Indian cheese with nuts, spicy meat chunks with cool yogurt dips for contrast - spinach and lamb in a garlic and tomato sauce, - seasonal vegetables, lightly cooked with cashew nuts, are just a few of the delights in store when dining at Anoki.

Anoki Restaurant.
The Old Picture Hall,
129 London Road, Derby
01332 292888. www.anoki.co.uk
Open everyday 5:30pm - 11:30pm

Masa
Derby

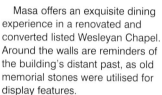

Masa offers an exquisite dining experience in a renovated and converted listed Wesleyan Chapel. Around the walls are reminders of the building's distant past, as old memorial stones were utilised for display features.

With its highly respected and growing reputation, Masa, owned by Didar and Paula Dalkic, really needs no further accolade. Intriguingly Masa is a Turkish word that simply means 'Table', and it couldn't be a more appropriate name, as Masa is all about the dining experience, nothing is taken away from the food, it's just you and your meal at your 'table'.

Dishes include 'Pan fried red Mullet' served with a tagliatelli of Crab.

'Spiced fillet of Monkfish' served on a bed of Puy lentils, with root vegetable and mussel chowder.

'Caramelised Banana tart tatin' served with toffee ice cream and 'Apple and Cinnamon tart' served with vanilla anglaise, maple syrup ice cream.

Restaurant is open seven days a week for lunch and dinner.
The Old Wesleyan Chapel,
Brook Street. Derby DE1 3PF
01332 203345
www.masarestaurantwinebar.com

Hudson Bay
Alfreton

Hudson Bay divides itself naturally into three areas, a smart bar where you can perch at high tables to enjoy a light lunch and a drink, a calm area to relax while finishing with a coffee and a restaurant where friendly bar staff serve a variety of menus throughout the week.

Lunchtime food and à là carte evening meals are available daily. With their menu's changing frequently there is always something new to try. Steaks are a speciality!

It is the small touches that make a meal and the glass jug of iced water, which without asking arrives with your wine, and the generous portion of butter in a white bowl, and the slices of home baked cheese and date bread make all the difference.

A lunchtime drink and a sandwich provides the perfect break to the working day and at Hudson Bay you won't be disappointed.

Hudson Bay Bar & Restaurant,
32 Nottingham Road, Alfreton.
01773 546500.
www.hudson-bay.co.uk
Food served 7 days
12 - 3pm, 6 - 9pm.
Sunday Lunch 12 - 3pm

Marquis of Ormonde
Codnor

The Marquis of Ormonde has been run by Dave and Sally Dawes for about four years.

The Marquis of Ormonde has so much to offer. First on the list of course is the food and drink. There is a steak night, a carvery, a fish night, lunchtime specials Monday to Saturday and of course Sunday lunch.

It is also a drinking establishment and you will feel at home here if you are not going to eat but want to enjoy the guest beers in the friendly atmosphere. . . There are indoor skittles available and a pool table. Quiz night is also very popular with a free supper and cash snowball prizes.

The function room at the Marquis of Ormond is ideal for parties, anniversaries and business meetings.

The Marquis of Ormonde is the place to go for a great pint, home cooked food, generous portions and super value.

Marquis of Ormonde.
Codnor Denby Lane, Codnor.
01773 742607
Food served Evenings:
Tuesday - Saturday 6-9pm
Lunchtimes:
Monday - Saturday 12-2.30pm
Sunday 12-3pm

The Saracens Head
Shirley

Picture the scene - log fires burning, an oak table with the candle flickering gently in the centre.

The chef at The Saracens Head, Scott Heath, has over 20 years experience as a master chef. Scott's menu hangs over the fire on a blackboard, and is refreshed frequently to keep abreast of local and seasonal produce.

The menu includes:
Roast Tomato and Pepper Soup with melting cheese profiterole and two home baked sun dried tomato rolls, with butter. Smoked Halibut Souffle with home cured gin and tonic salmon. Rib of local Beef, onion and mushroom pie with Old Trip gravy, mustard mash and sauteed peas.

Puddings are off the Specials Board and include White Chocolate and Coconut Cheesecake, encased in chocolate.

A lunch menu includes ciabatta sandwiches, for example: roasted peppers and goats cheese or hot beef, horseradish and onion.

Food served 12-2.30, 6.30-9pm.
Closed Tuesday.
Open all day Sunday
01335 360330
Shirley, Ashbourne.

Archie's
Sandiacre

Archie's restaurant finds its beginning in an old barn at the rear of an early 1900's butchers shop. The barn, though, has been lovingly and tastefully restored to become home for Sandiacre's newest place to eat. Lloyd and Rebecca Pearson immediately saw the potential to realise their dream of opening their own restaurant.

Archie's award winning Head Chef Ian Matthews, along with his team, offer exciting dishes from around the world, and boast locally supplied, fresh produce.

The co-owner Lloyd Pearson and head-chef Ian Mathews are qualified chefs, having experience of hotels and restaurants around the country.

On the menu are delights such as: Pan fried mussels in a wine and cream sauce, with dry cured bacon and shallots.

Herb crusted rack of Derbyshire lamb, Baileys bread & butter pudding with butterscotch sauce!

Food served
Tuesday - Saturday 5pm - 10pm.
Sunday Carvery 11.30 - 3pm.
The Barn, Bridge Street, Sandiacre.
01159 499 324

The White Bear
Stretton

The White Bear, an old Derbyshire stone inn, charmingly rustic with exposed stone walls, scrubbed tables, flagged floors, low beams and a patchwork of rooms off the bar, creating cosy, informal dining areas. It is along the ridge between Higham and Clay Cross. It is tucked in the corner made by the lane which sneaks off down towards Ashover.

Jason and Stephanie extend a traditional warm welcome to their guests. Awards and accolades have followed Jason wherever he has worked since 1993, and the menu has the mark of an experienced chef.

Jason uses a huge variety of ingredients, including some more unusual ones such as palm-sugar (used in the Spiced Duck dressing,) and creates beautiful sauces and vegetables as accompaniments.

Prices start from £4.75 for starters, from £10.95 for mains and from £4.50 for desserts. Wine starts from £10.50 a bottle.

The White Bear
is open for lunch and for dinner.
Main Road, Stretton.
01246 863274

Complete the taste experience...

Moving into a new house?
Restoring a traditional property?

The place to head for is The Glory Hole where you'll find an interesting selection of old and new furniture and accessories.

The Glory Hole is owned and run by Colin and Debbie Reid who share a love of quality and traditional interiors. They started the business in 1984 gradually changing from just dealing in antique furniture to restoring and then producing quality bespoke items to order. Now this side has completely taken over, customers can have their own ideas and designs created and installed, no two kitchens are the same!

Colin is responsible for the design, manufacture and installation of the kitchens and fireplaces made at his factory in Sawley, Notts. They are proud of their staff who are all highly trained and talented when it comes to producing bespoke, all

A recently designed and fitted Glory Hole kitchen

Colin & Debbie at The Glory Hole

timber furniture, kitchens and fire surrounds, freestanding or fitted no chipboard is used in construction whatsoever! Installation includes all necessary gas, electrical, plumbing and carpentry work undertaken by The Glory Hole staff. Additionally, Colin and Debbie have converted the old Barn at the rear of the Glory Hole into the licensed restaurant called 'Archie's'. So if you are looking for inspiration, why not visit the shop in Sandiacre, there are 8 rooms of occasional furniture, lamps, mirrors, tables and chairs, radiator covers, bookcases, wardrobes etc. Plus a wide range of cabinet and door fittings. The shop is situated close to The Erewash Canal and in the shadow of Springfield Mill.

The Glory Hole

14 – 16 Station Road, Sandiacre, Notts, NG10 5BG   Tel: 0115 939 4081 Fax: 0115 939 4085

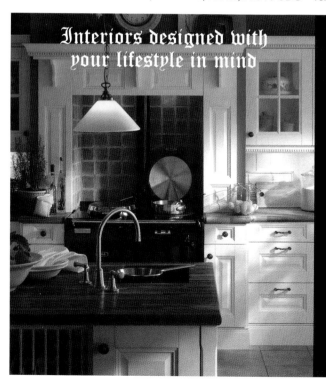

Taste fresh produce at the farmers' markets

Errata

Pages 92 & 93

Bloomers Original Bakewell Pudding Recipe
Serves 6

Ingredients
6 to 8oz Puff Paste 'Pastry'
4 to 6oz Sieved Strawberry Jam
4oz Caster Sugar
6 Eggs
3oz Unsalted Butter
4oz Ground Almonds
A Touch of Almond Essence

Method
1. Roll out the pastry, line the shallow pie dish, prick the base.
2. Cover the base with the jam.
3. Melt the butter.
4. Separate the eggs, use only the yolks.
5. Beat together all the ingredients; pour in the melted butter last. You will have a smooth batter mixture.
6. Pour the filling over the jam.
7. Bake at Mark 5 or 6, 175°C, 300°F or to suit the oven, for 30 minutes or until golden brown.
8. Serve warm with fresh cream.

Pages 96 & 97

Derbyshire Honey Fruit Cake
Serves 12

Ingredients
227g/ 8oz self-raising flour
113g/ 4oz butter
56g/ 2oz peel
113g/ 4oz sultanas
227g/ 8oz Derbyshire Clear Honey
113g/ 4oz currents
2 eggs
Pinch of nutmeg and salt
3 tablespoons of milk

Method
1. Cream honey and butter together.
2. Beat eggs well and add alternately with sifted flour, nutmeg and salt. Add fruit, peel etc. Beat well and lightly, adding milk.
3. Bake in well buttered 180mm/ 7inch tin and bake in a moderate oven for 2-3 hours.